MARCIA DECOSTER'S
BEADED OPULENCE

MARCIA DECOSTER'S

BEADED OPULENCE

ELEGANT JEWELRY PROJECTS WITH RIGHT ANGLE WEAVE

LARK BOOKS

A Division of Sterling Publishing Co., Inc.
New York / London

Senior Editor
Ray Hemachandra

Editor
Nathalie Mornu

Art Director
Dana Irwin

Photographer
Stewart O'Shields

Cover Designer
Celia Naranjo

Library of Congress Cataloging-in-Publication Data

DeCoster, Marcia.
  Marcia DeCoster's beaded opulence : elegant jewelry projects with right angle weave / Marcia DeCoster. -- 1st ed.
      p. cm.
   Includes index.
   ISBN 978-1-60059-292-8 (hc-plc with jacket : alk. paper)
   1. Beadwork. 2. Jewelry making. I. Title. II. Title: Beaded opulence.
   TT860.D424 2009
   739.27--dc22
                                                        2008050857
   10 9 8 7 6 5 4 3 2

Published by Lark Books, A Division of
Sterling Publishing Co., Inc.
387 Park Avenue South, New York, NY 10016

Text and illustrations © 2009, Marcia DeCoster
Photography © 2009, Lark Books, unless otherwise specified
Photography on pages 16, 69, and 103 © 2009 Marcia DeCoster

Distributed in Canada by Sterling Publishing,
c/o Canadian Manda Group, 165 Dufferin Street
Toronto, Ontario, Canada M6K 3H6

Distributed in the United Kingdom by GMC Distribution Services,
Castle Place, 166 High Street, Lewes, East Sussex, England BN7 1XU

Distributed in Australia by Capricorn Link (Australia) Pty Ltd.,
P.O. Box 704, Windsor, NSW 2756 Australia

The written instructions, photographs, designs, patterns, and projects in this volume are intended for the personal use of the reader and may be reproduced for that purpose only. Any other use, especially commercial use, is forbidden under law without written permission of the copyright holder.

Every effort has been made to ensure that all the information in this book is accurate. However, due to differing conditions, tools, and individual skills, the publisher cannot be responsible for any injuries, losses, and other damages that may result from the use of the information in this book.

If you have questions or comments about this book, please contact:
Lark Books
67 Broadway
Asheville, NC 28801
828-253-0467

Manufactured in China

ISBN 13: 978-1-60059-292-8

For information about custom editions, special sales, and premium and corporate purchases, please contact the Sterling Special Sales Department at 800-805-5489 or specialsales@sterlingpub.com.

CONTENTS

INTRODUCTION

TINY, WONDERFUL BEADS, THOSE TWINKLING OBJECTS OF DESIRE—I'M CRAZY ABOUT THEM! I LOVE TO COLLECT THEM, I LOVE TO FONDLE THEM, AND I *REALLY* LOVE TO TURN THEM INTO GORGEOUS JEWELRY.

I've always wanted to create with my hands, and after working in different media over the years, I discovered beadweaving. The variety of beadweaving stitches and the rich abundance of bead colors, shapes, and finishes provided the perfect amount of stimulation. I had found my passion. Although I've become proficient in many stitches, I keep gravitating back to right angle weave. Its amazing versatility enables me to make pieces that satisfy both my desire for personal adornment and my quest for ever more elaborate design.

I've separated this book into chapters, each exploring a different way of working with right angle weave. Within every chapter, I've loosely arranged the projects in order of complexity, and the projects all include several fundamental techniques so you can improve your skills as you weave beautiful designs. But first, look over the Fundamentals chapter. You'll need a base set of skills for your beading journey, so I give you a comprehensive understanding of how to work single-needle right angle weave. I cover working flat, tubular, increases, decreases, and shaping, as well as more advanced techniques such as repairing, fashioning curves, and embellishing.

The basic right angle stitch, without shaping or embellishment, produces a supple fabric that takes on the form of whatever it's draped over. Projects in the Fabric chapter showcase this quality. Spun Glass (page 31), for example, hugs the wrist for a perfect, sparkling fit. Right angle weave ropes are quite flexible, too, just the thing for necklaces, bracelets, and anklets. The Ropes chapter contains great designs for showing off a favorite focal bead or incorporating unusual beads, like the irregular, elongated pearls used as the bottom beads of the right angle weave unit for the Ka'iulani anklet on page 48. Tubular right angle weave, meanwhile, is an ideal method for covering armatures; in the third chapter, you'll learn how to cover a bangle or create interesting shapes such as the classical teardrop pendant in Etruscan Treasure (page 60).

The Embellishments chapter focuses on one of the most exciting features of right angle weave—the ability to add beads between the spaces created in the base fabric. This characteristic offers endless opportunities to add both visual interest and give structure. The beadwork embellishing Cappadocia (page 72) gives this cuff a flared shape, lending extra glint and glimmer to the tilted fire-polished beads of the base fabric. The Curves chapter introduces some of the many ways of shaping. And in the final chapter, I expose you to different ways of building layers. The burnished gold and jewel-toned Amphora bead (page 106) is first embellished, and then additional layers of right angle weave get added between the embellished rows.

The many projects I offer here will let you explore the versatility of right angle weave. So gather your beads, fondle them and let them trickle through your fingers as you consider colors and design variations, and then bring your own creative voice to the jewelry by being inventive in your choices. And when you're ready, be inspired by the stitch to create your own designs.

9

CHAPTER ONE

BASIC BEADING KIT

ONE OF THE GREAT PLEASURES OF TEACHING IS GETTING EXPOSED TO THE VARIOUS MATERIALS AND TOOLS that other beaders use. In this way, I've discovered countless creative ways to use ordinary implements to assist the beading process. Over the years, I've assembled my own list of favorites to include in a basic beading kit.

Beads

Beads come in a vast variety of materials, finishes, sizes, and shapes. As I come across them, I buy any new finishes and colors that appeal to me so my design choices are immediately at hand when I'm creating.

Seed Beads

In the majority of my beadweaving designs I begin with a base of Japanese seed beads. The sizes I predominantly use are 15°, 11°, and 8°, with 15° being the smallest and 8° the largest. I love all of the finishes and colors of seed beads, including the wonderful matte metallic, metallic, silver-lined, and opaque beads.

Crystal Beads

I love sparkle in my beadwork! To achieve this, I use various shapes of Austrian crystals, including bicones, rounds, and teardrops. Another of my favorite crystal shapes, the rivoli, is a large faceted crystal that can be bezeled with seed beads. Also available are Austrian crystal pearls—they are very uniform and a nice addition to your beadweaving supply list.

Fire-Polished Beads

Many of my designs include fire-polished beads. They are made in the Czech Republic and are known for their light-catching facets.

Lampworked Beads

Lampworked beads are handmade glass beads worked over a flame. They work well as inspiration and a focal point for a design.

Thread

There are six main types of beading thread used over and over again by beaders.

Nymo

Nymo is a monofilament nylon thread in size A (thin) and D (thicker) that's used in the upholstery industry. It comes in a wide assortment of colors. I find that students have a tendency to shred this thread when doing right angle weave with small beads, so beginners might want to select a different thread.

Silamide

Silamide, a pre-waxed twisted filament, is also used in the upholstery industry. It's strong and has less of a tendency to shred, but it can snap and is easily cut by the sharp edges of crystals. Color selection is somewhat limited.

C-Lon

C-Lon is another nylon thread that's stronger than Nymo, but I find that it, too, has a tendency to shred when doing right angle weave with small beads.

One G

One G, manufactured by ToHo, is a very strong beading thread. Color selection is somewhat limited, but the bobbin size makes it a very portable thread—perfect for carry-along seed bead projects.

K.O.

K.O. thread is quite strong and a good alternative to Nymo. It comes pre-waxed, and is resistant to abrasion and tangles.

Braided Beading Thread

Braided beading thread is actually a fishing line that works great for off-loom beadwork. It comes in two colors (smoke and crystal) and in multiple weights, and is very strong. It's a good choice for any project using crystals, which have a tendency to cut other thread choices. I find the 6-pound weight to be a good choice for most projects. The smoke color easily blends with most dark-colored beads, while the crystal works well for light or metallic palettes such as gold and silver. This type of thread can "cut" itself when knotted, but because most right angle weave knots are done over 2 to 4 strands of thread and don't carry a lot of tension, I haven't experienced this problem.

Tip: Some braided beading threads have a graphite coating that can be messy on your hands. To remedy this, simply fold a piece of paper towel over the thread and pull the length through the towel several times to remove the graphite.

Thread Treatments

There are three main products I like to use to prepare my thread for stitching.

Thread Heaven

Thread Heaven is a commercially prepared thread conditioner used for detangling threads.

Waxes

Microcrystalline wax and beeswax are used to coat and stiffen thread. These products help make thread more manageable, especially when working with it doubled. Microcrystalline wax tends to be less sticky than beeswax and is my favorite choice.

Hand Tools

I always keep these tools within reach while I'm beading. I consider them to be an integral part of any good beadweaving tool set.

Beading Needles

Most seed bead projects are easily accomplished with a size 12 beading needle. If you're stitching with charlottes or size 15° seed beads, it may be necessary to use a size 13 needle; it's smaller than the 12 and allows for multiple passes through the beads. In small, tight spaces a "sharp"—a shorter and stiffer beading needle—can be really useful.

Scissors

I use a small pair of sharp embroidery scissors to cut most everything. Braided beading thread, however, is best cut with inexpensive scissors because it has a tendency to dull blades. Most beaders carry a pair of children's scissors for this purpose. If you don't wish to travel with scissors, a handy cutting tool on the market is a round razor blade encased with metal and notched at intervals.

Pliers/Needle Pull

You may occasionally have trouble pulling your needle through beads with thread-filled holes. Although using your teeth can be tempting, your dentist would definitely not consider this a good solution! While a pair of chain-nose pliers does the job, I was recently introduced to a needle pull—a small piece of surgical tubing. When wrapped around the needle, the latex "grabs" the metal so it won't slip out of your fingers as you pull the needle through the hole.

Awl

A small diameter awl can be a great tool for coaxing a wayward bead into place or removing a knot.

Tweezers

Tweezers are a good tool for removing knots. The two pointed ends can be placed inside the knot; when the tweezers are pulled apart, so is the knot.

Additional Tools

I'm happiest working at a table in my studio, basking in natural daylight, and surrounded by my supplies of beads, tools, and inspiration. There are times when this isn't practical, however, so I have to improvise to create an optimal working space. This includes good light, a comfortable chair, a table, close access to my tools, and a velvet pad as my beading surface. If I must work from my lap, I place a pillow under the beading pad to bring it closer to my hands.

Task Light

If you like to travel with your beadwork, a portable full-spectrum light will help prevent eyestrain in poorly lit places. Bring an extension cord so you can plug in anyplace.

Beading Surface

The majority of my students use a velvety nylon fabric mat (think hotel blankets) as their working surface. Look for a mat that's lightweight, portable, and easy to store. I prefer to bead from a leather tray, ½ inch (1.3 cm) high and lined with a velvet pad. I have several in both light blue and black and choose the appropriate color based on the type of beads I'm using.

Still other beaders use sectioned ceramic trays to keep their beads from mixing. I tend toward messiness as a beader, and my beads always end up in a glittery, succulent pile.

Needle Case

Needle cases make your needles easy to find. They come in many different shapes, but one of my favorites is a cylindrical box whose lid stays in place with friction. Beaders often cover their needle cases in beadwork.

Scoops

There are many scoops available for picking up beads and returning them to their containers. Although my palettes often continue to live on in their respective beading trays, I use a baby spoon when I need to pick up beads.

Scrap Container

It's handy to have some sort of vessel for throwing away odd bits of thread or culled beads. My personal favorite is a fabric basket attached to a weighted pincushion where I sometimes stash my beading needles. I hang the basket from the edge of the table so it stays out of the way, keeping my work area neat and my needles nearby.

13

CHAPTER TWO

FUNDAMENTALS

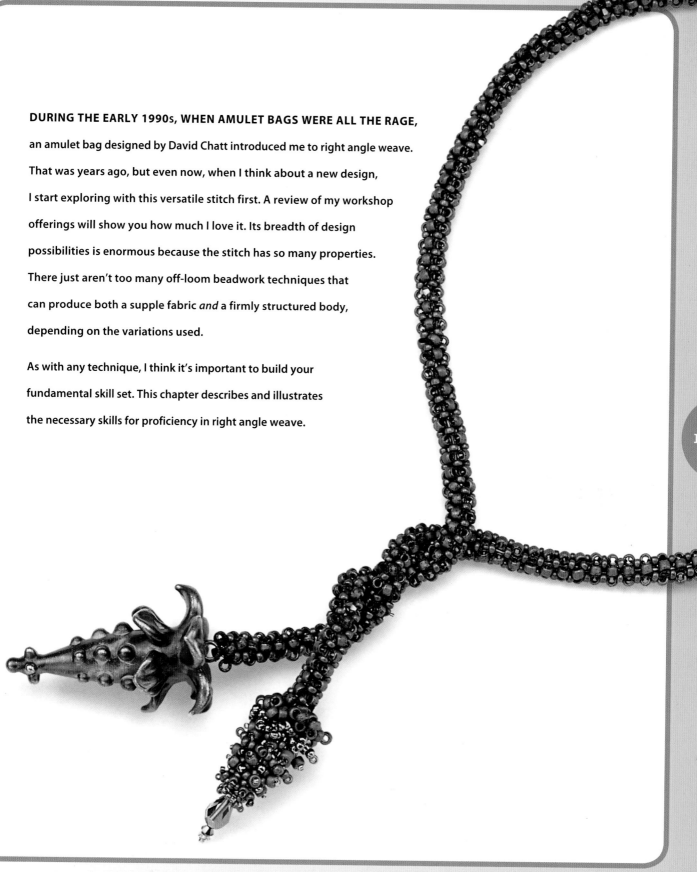

DURING THE EARLY 1990s, WHEN AMULET BAGS WERE ALL THE RAGE,
an amulet bag designed by David Chatt introduced me to right angle weave.
That was years ago, but even now, when I think about a new design,
I start exploring with this versatile stitch first. A review of my workshop
offerings will show you how much I love it. Its breadth of design
possibilities is enormous because the stitch has so many properties.
There just aren't too many off-loom beadwork techniques that
can produce both a supple fabric *and* a firmly structured body,
depending on the variations used.

As with any technique, I think it's important to build your
fundamental skill set. This chapter describes and illustrates
the necessary skills for proficiency in right angle weave.

Terminology

The beads that make up the 4 sides of a right angle weave stitch sit at right angles to one another. It's this property that makes for both a very flexible and a very versatile stitch. The thread running between each of the 4 sides creates a fluid fabric that can bend in any direction.

That fluid quality is a great plus, but because the beads all sit in different directions it can be tricky to convey this technique in writing. So, when using this book, take note of the terms I use when writing about this stitch:

- A right angle weave stitch has 4 "sides" that make up a unit. I think of these as the top, bottom, and sides.

- A right angle weave unit is usually just made up of 1 top, 1 bottom, and 2 side beads, basically forming a square. In the instructions, you can assume that a unit is 4 beads around unless I note otherwise.

- For the first row of right angle weave beadwork, the first and all subsequent units share a side with the next unit. In the second and all subsequent rows, the top beads of the previous row's units are the bottom beads of the current row's units. Keep in mind that top and bottom are relative, depending on how you're holding your beadwork.

- I bead "up," from left to right on odd rows, and right to left on even rows, so the project directions are written that way. This is my personal choice, but many beaders choose to flip their work over at the end of each row so they're always beading in the same direction.

- I focus on single-needle right angle weave in this book, but each of the projects can be done with two-needle right angle weave. This technique, sometimes called "cross-needle weaving," is done by working with one needle on each end of the thread. Instead of working in clockwise and counterclockwise circles, the threads cross through beads to make the units.

- The term *pass through* means your needle enters the bead hole the same way it was strung. *Pass back through* refers to entering the bead in the opposite direction from which it was strung.

Once you've developed your skills, you can make any number of variations to the Beaded Bangle project (page 52).

16

Considering Thread

Thread…Single? Double? Waxed? Length? Again, all of these are personal choices, but here are my road-tested guidelines for dealing with your thread.

Single or Double Thread

In right angle weave you make multiple passes through your beads, creating a sort of beaded fabric. If you want a piece to achieve a very drapey, silky feel, opt for working with a single thread. If you're adding embellishments to a piece, especially those with sharp holes, or if the piece needs to maintain a firm structure, then choose doubled thread. The decision also needs to be made based on the size of beads you're using: If the piece calls for size 15° seed beads with embellishments, you may need to go with single thread in order to pass through the small beads multiple times.

Waxing and Thread Type

If you're using doubled thread, waxing it will tame the unruliness of the two strands. For single thread, it's not that important to wax. In this book, I consider both thread choice and wax to be personal preferences except in a few cases, where I recommend a particular thread type for best results.

Thread Length

If you're working on a large project, start with a wingspan length of thread. If you're working with doubled thread for that large project, use two wingspans and then double it. By using this amount of thread—not too much, not too little—you'll increase your beading speed by reducing both the number of tangles and the amount of pulls you need to get the thread through your beads.

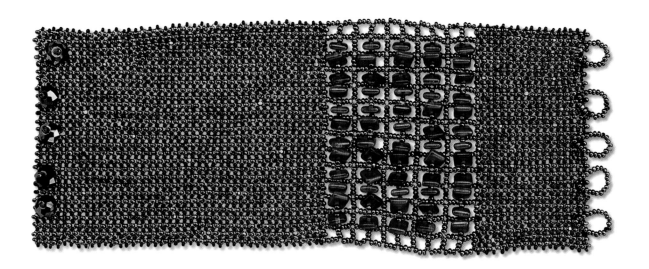

Flat Right Angle Weave

This technique produces a flat piece of beadwork. Work the rows back and forth, unit by unit.

Tip: While learning right angle weave, it's helpful to use two contrasting-color beads. Use one color for the top and bottom beads and one for the side beads of each unit.

Pick up 4 beads. Tie the beads into a circle using an overhand knot. Pass through the first bead strung. Orient your work so the bead you just passed through is a right-hand side bead (figure 1).

Pick up 3 beads. Moving counterclockwise, pass through the side bead you just exited, the first bead just strung (the bottom bead) and the second bead just strung (the new side bead).
Note: You'll always pass through the new side bead before beginning another right angle weave unit (figure 2).

Pick up 3 beads. Traveling clockwise this time, pass through the side bead you just exited, and the top and side bead just added (figure 3).

Pick up 3 beads. Moving counterclockwise, pass through the bead you just exited, and the bottom and side beads just added (figure 4). Note how every other group of beads alternates direction from clockwise to counterclockwise.

To begin a new row, you must pass through a top bead of the current row. I call this "stepping up." If you're traveling counterclockwise, you'll pass through the bottom bead, the side bead, and then the top bead (figure 5). (If you're moving clockwise, then you only need to pass

through the top bead before continuing, as in figure 5a. If the second unit was counterclockwise, as shown in figure 2, then all even units will be counterclockwise and all odd units will be clockwise.)

Add 3 beads. Moving clockwise, pass through the top bead from the right and continue through the side bead (figure 6). The first unit of row 2 and each subsequent row always begins by adding a side, a top, and a side bead.

figure 1

figure 2

figure 3

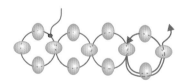

figure 4

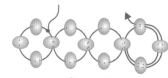

figure 5

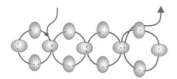

figure 5a

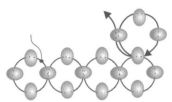

figure 6

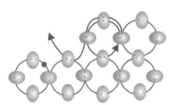

figure 7

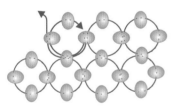

figure 8

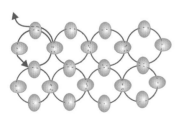

figure 9

Add 2 beads. Working counterclockwise, pass through the top bead of the next row 1 unit, from left to right. Continue through the side bead of the first unit in this row and the new top and side beads just added. Pass through the top bead of the following row 1 unit from right to left (figure 7). The second and all subsequent units require only 2 new beads. A top bead from the previous row and a side bead from the previous unit are shared beads.

Add 2 beads. Traveling clockwise, pass through the side bead from the previous unit. Continue through the top bead of the previous row and the new side bead (figure 8).

Add 2 beads. Moving counterclockwise, pass through the top bead of the next row 1 unit and the side bead of the previous unit. Because this is the last unit in this row, pass through only the top bead to begin the next row (figure 9). **Note:** If your last unit was made in a clockwise direction, you'll need to pass through 3 beads to position your thread to exit from the top bead.

You may find it more comfortable to flip your work at the end of each row so you're always working left to right or right to left, depending on your preference.

Tip: Sometimes while weaving or embellishing you'll find you need to secure the tension on the working thread before moving on to the next step. Do this by making a half-hitch knot on the threads between the beads, adjacent to the working thread. This is especially helpful when working a project such as Urchin (page 83). This technique also works well for changing thread path direction while beading. Just make a half-hitch knot between beads and pass back through a bead to exit in the desired direction.

19

Counting Units

To count units, tally the bottom beads of each 4-sided unit in a row. To count rows, add up the side beads along the edge (figure 10).

Adding Length or Width

You can easily add length or width to any of the 4 sides of your existing piece. Just use your needle to weave your thread through adjacent beads to the place you want to add more units, and begin working right angle weave along the edge (figures 11 and 12).

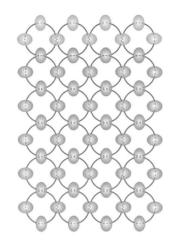

figure 11

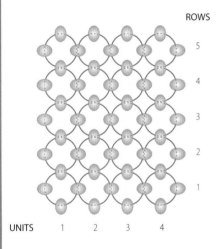

ROWS

5

4

3

2

1

UNITS   1   2   3   4

figure 10

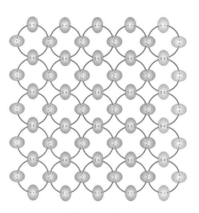

figure 12

Changing Bead Counts

The beads that make up the 4 sides of a unit can be any count, size, or type (figure 13). This is a great aspect of right angle weave, because it gives you the opportunity to make a dense or lacy fabric of beads. ***Note:*** When you use multiple beads on a side, they're treated as 1 bead, in that you pass through them all at once.

Shaping

You can add shape to right angle weave fabric by changing the number or size of beads per side. For example, when you use a size 15° seed bead as a bottom bead and size 11° seed beads for the sides and top, you introduce a curve. To make the curve even more pronounced, you might add 2 size 11° beads in each unit's top position (figure 14). To create smooth curves, make increases gradually in successive rows.

Another method of shaping a piece of right angle weave is to pass the thread through adjacent vertically or horizontally oriented beads without adding any extra beads between. When you pull the thread tight, the beadwork curves. This can be done along an edge, as shown in figure 15, or you can do this within the beaded fabric, creating a nice gather.

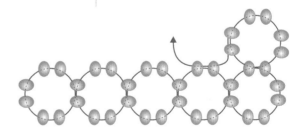

figure 13

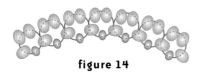

figure 14

figure 15

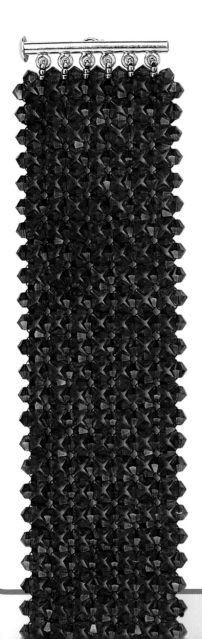

Beginning and Ending Threads

When you have 6 to 8 inches (15.2 to 20.3 cm) of working thread left in a project, you need to add more. To do so, cut a new length of thread and pass through a bead several units away from where you left off. Follow the right angle weave thread path you just completed, making half-hitch knots between beads at two points along the way, until you reach the bead last exited. Place a needle on the old thread and weave through the beads, following the right angle weave thread path and tying knots between beads to secure it. Trim the old thread close to the beadwork and resume working with the new thread (figure 16).

Tip: I strive to make all my beadwork so it maintains its integrity over time, but broken threads and missing beads do happen. At the end of every project I put together a "repair" kit with several of each of the beads used in the design. Even though repairs are some years away, this precaution makes it very easy to find the right beads should a mending job become necessary.

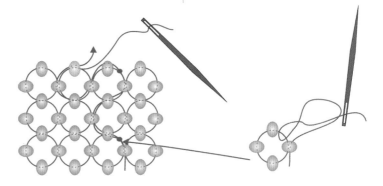

figure 16

Tubular Right Angle Weave

This technique makes a beaded tube or rope. There are two ways to do it: one you work in rounds, and the other you work flat and join into a tube.

Working in Rounds

Make a strip the number of desired units, minus one. Bring the side beads at the ends of the row together so they sit side by side. Make a right angle weave stitch, adding a top and bottom bead. The join creates the additional unit. To begin the second round, pass through a top bead in the first round, pick up 3 beads, and pass through the top bead (figure 17).

Continue round 2 as usual. When you have 1 unit left, pick up 1 bead, pass through the side bead from the first unit, the top bead of the previous row, the side bead of the last unit, and back through the top bead just added (figure 18). **Note:** The order of beads will depend on the direction you are traveling. If you worked the last unit counterclockwise, you'll pass through the top bead of the previous row and the side bead of the first unit. Then you'll pick up 1 bead and pass through the side bead of the last unit.

Working Flat and Joining

Another way to form a tube is by stitching a piece of flat right angle weave and then joining two opposite edges. This technique works especially well if you're covering an armature with beadwork. In general, I'm most comfortable working flat and then joining, but this is just my own preference.

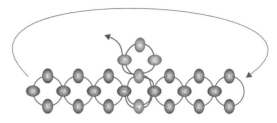

figure 17

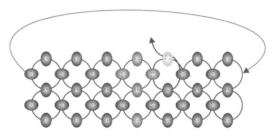

figure 18

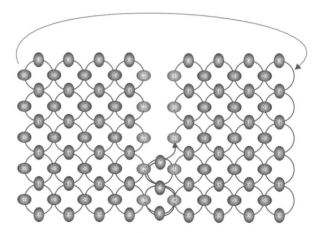

figure 19

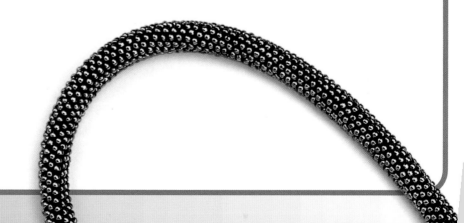

To work a tube with this method, make a strip of right angle weave to the desired length and 1 unit less than the desired width. When complete, fold the two edges to be joined so their side beads match. Position your thread so it exits down through a side bead. Pick up a bottom bead and pass through the opposing side bead. Pick up a top bead and pass down through the side bead first exited. Pass through the new bottom bead, up through the opposing side bead, the new top bead, and up through the side bead of the next unit. Pick up a top bead and pass down through the opposing side bead. Continue passing through the bottom bead, up through the side bead, the new top bead, and up through the side bead of the next unit. Repeat until all units are joined. The join creates an additional unit (figure 19).

One design consideration to keep in mind while working tubular right angle weave is the number of odd or even spaces in the finished tube's rounds. This point is especially important when making surface embellishments to a tube, because an even unit count is essential to an alternating fringe or other evenly spaced decoration (such as in Ringlets, page 66). So when you start with your first row of right angle weave, whether you're working flat or in the round, remember that if you start the row with an odd number of units, you'll end up with an even number of units once you join the ends.

Joining

Joining may be used in a number of techniques. It can join a flat piece of right angle weave into a tube, as in figure 19, or fasten two separate pieces of right angle weave together (figure 20). It can also connect embellishment beads to make additional layers of right angle weave on the surface of a piece, as in the projects in the Layers chapter.

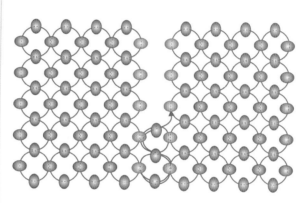

figure 20

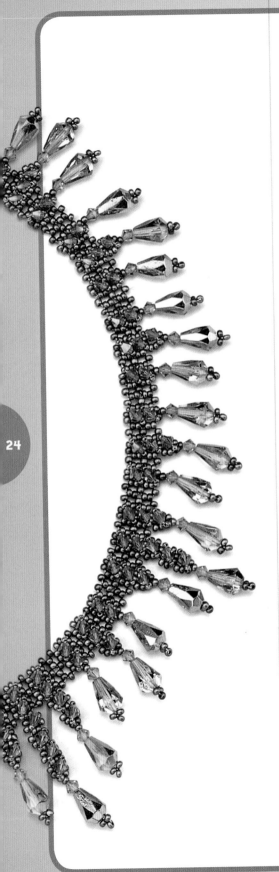

Embellishing

The space created within each right angle weave unit is a natural place to embellish your beadwork. Because the bead holes run both horizontally and vertically, you can easily exit 1 bead in the piece, pick up 1 bead, and pass through the next similarly oriented bead in the row. Embellishing offers another chance for shaping beadwork: Adding a smaller bead than those used on the base will bring the base beads closer together; adding one of the same size will add structure, but not shape; and a larger bead will force apart the base beads, creating a curve in the base fabric. Finally, fringe and right angle weave are great partners—it's up to you to explore the infinite possibilities (figure 21)

Tip: When weaving or embellishing with beads that have sharp edges (such as crystals), be sure to pull the thread parallel with the bead holes rather than at an angle. Pulling it at an angle may cause abrasion or breakage.

Increasing

To make a mid-row increase with your thread exiting up through a side bead, pick up 3 beads instead of the 2 beads you'd usually add to make a mid-row unit. Pass through the side bead just exited without passing through the top bead of the previous row. Pass through the new top and side beads and work across the row as usual. This will add 1 new unit to the row (figure 22).

You can also make an increase at the edge of a piece. Simply exit up through the side bead of the row you'd like to increase. Pick up 3 beads, pass through the side bead just exited, and through the new top and side beads. Repeat for as many units as you wish to increase (figure 23).

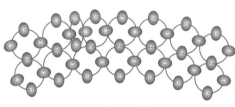

figure 22

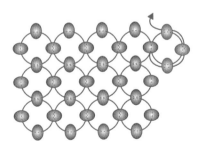

figure 21

figure 23

Decreasing

To make a mid-row decrease with your thread exiting up through a side bead, add 2 beads, skip the top bead of the previous row's next unit, and pass through the following one. You will now have 1 less unit in the subsequent row (figure 24).

To decrease at the end of a row, stop 1 unit short of ending the row (or however many units you want to decrease by), step up to the new row, and continue (figure 25).

To decrease at the beginning of a row, weave the thread through the beads to exit from the top bead of the unit where you wish to start the new row (figure 26).

Shortening and Cutting

If you need to shorten a piece of right angle weave but can't unweave the thread and beads, it's possible to trim it with a scissors. Before making the cut, reinforce the thread paths on each side of the problem area by passing through the beads many times. I find this easiest to do by adding a highly contrasting thread through each of the beads where the cut will occur. Next, I anchor two threads, one on each side of the contrasting thread, and reinforce the beads on both sides. The threads on each side of the contrasting thread can be cut afterward and the piece will retain its stitch integrity (figure 27). This technique is especially helpful on a project such as Beaded Bangle (page 52).

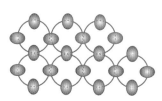

figure 24

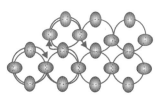

figure 25

figure 26

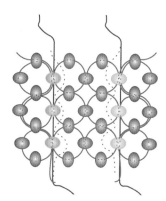

figure 27

CHAPTER THREE

FABRIC

ABACUS

Two sizes of beads form the textural fabric of this wide cuff.

The square accent beads woven into it add both color and visual interest,

while a simple closure complements the spare design.

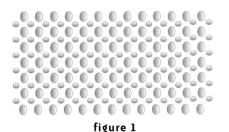

figure 1

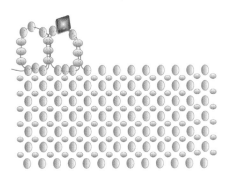

figure 2

▶ 1. Base

Rows 1–41: Work a strip of right angle weave 28 units wide and 41 units long. Use size 15° beads for the sides of each unit and size 11° beads for the tops and bottoms (figure 1).

Row 42: Pass through the top size 11° bead of the last unit in row 41. Pick up 1 size 11° bead and pass through the next size 11° bead in row 41. Pick up 9 (3 side, 3 top, and 3 side) size 11° beads and pass through the original size 11° bead, the bead you added between the 2 top beads of the previous row, and the next bead. Pass up through the 3 side beads to begin the next unit. Repeat across, but on the second through twelfth units replace the middle bead of the top 3 beads with a squarelette bead. The fourteenth unit will be completed with all seed beads as in unit 1 (figure 2).

Continued on next page

SUPPLIES

Basic Beading Kit (page 10)

**Dark gray matte size 15°
seed beads, 7 g**

**Hematite size 11° charlotte
seed beads, 22 g**

**60 hot pink top-drilled glass
squarelette beads, 6 mm**

**5 hematite crystal rondelles,
8 x 5 mm**

Row 43: Work the units using 3 size 11° beads for each side and top (figure 3).

Rows 44: Work the first unit using all size 11° beads. Stitch the second through twelfth units using 3 size 11° beads for each side and 1 size 11° bead/1 square-lette/1 size 11° bead for the tops. Work the final unit with all size 11° beads.

Rows 45–52: Repeat rows 43 and 44 for a total of 8 rows.

Row 53: Weave through the beads to exit from the first top seed bead at the edge of row 52, toward the center. Pick up 1 size 15° bead, 1 size 11° bead, and 1 size 15° bead. Pass through the size 11° bead last exited and the first size 15° bead just added to make a unit. Pick up 1 size 11° bead and 1 size 15° bead, skip the next top bead of the last unit in the previous row, and pass back through the next one, the size 15° bead last exited, the 2 beads just added, and the first bead of the next set of top beads from the previous row. Continue across, using this bead pattern to work right angle weave off the first and third top beads of each row 52 unit to make a total of 28 units (figure 4).

Rows 54-69: Repeat row 53 for a total of 16 rows.

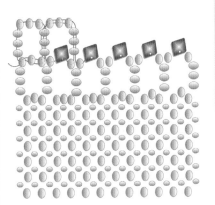

figure 3

figure 4

figure 5

▶ **2. Closure**

Weave through the beads to exit from the top bead of the fifth unit in row 67. Pick up 18 size 11° beads and pass through the bead you last exited to make a loop. Repeat the thread path to reinforce the loop. Weave through the beadwork to exit from the top bead of the tenth unit in that same row. Add a second matching loop. Continue adding loops on every fifth unit until there are a total of 5 loops (figure 5). Weave in the thread and trim.

Start a new thread that exits from the top bead of the fifth unit in row 3 (at the other end of the base). Pick up 1 rondelle and 1 size 11° bead. Pass back through the rondelle and the size 11° bead you originally exited. Repeat the thread path to reinforce the rondelle. Weave through the beads until you exit the top bead of the tenth unit in that same row. Add a second rondelle. Continue adding 1 rondelle to every fifth unit until there are a total of 5 rondelles (figure 6). Weave in the thread and trim.

figure 6

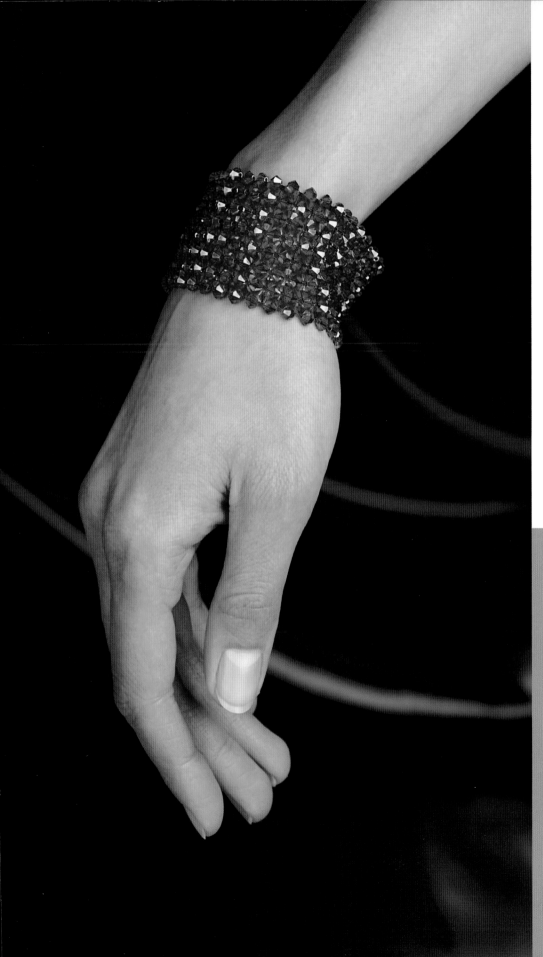

SPUN GLASS

The shape of the bicones allows them to nestle neatly into one another, so they lend themselves nicely to right angle weave. Pick a dazzling color, and the simplicity of this cuff will make its own statement each time you wear it.

SUPPLIES

Basic Beading Kit (page 10)

Smoke 6-pound braided beading thread

472 Siam AB2X bicone crystals, 4 mm

Metallic silver size 15° seed beads, < 0.5 g

Sterling silver 6-loop slide clasp, 36 mm

▶ 1. Base

Use doubled thread and the bicone crystals to work a strip of right angle weave 7 units wide and 31 rows long, or long enough to fit around your wrist minus ½ inch (1.3 cm) for the clasp.

▶ 2. Clasp

Orient the base so the last row (the short edge) points up. Weave through the beads to exit up through the inner side bead of the last unit added. Pick up 7 size 15° beads and pass through the clasp's first loop. Pass back through the bicone crystal you last exited and weave through the beads to exit up through the side bead of the next unit. Repeat to attach all 6 loops to one half of the clasp. Repeat on the other end of the bracelet (figure 1).

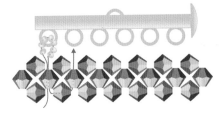

figure 1

SUPPLIES

Basic Beading Kit (page 10)

Size 8° seed beads:
    Matte olive AB, 5 g
    Bronze, 5 g

Size 11° seed beads:
    Matte purple luster, 2 g
    Metallic purple AB, 2 g
    Fuchsia-lined light
    amethyst, 1 g
    Bronze, 2 g

2-mm amethyst triangle
beads, 2 g

40 light Colorado topaz bicone
crystal beads, 4 mm

20 light amethyst bicone
crystal beads, 3 mm

30 bronze fire-polished
beads, 3 mm

Size 15° seed beads:
    Bronze, 1 g
    Fuchsia-lined light
    amethyst, 1 g

1 tabac square crystal
rivoli, 20 mm

1 dark bronze tab and bar
sewing closure, 18 mm

33

TWILIGHT

**This artful cuff uses assorted bead shapes and sizes to create a gently
draped right angle weave fabric. It gathers tastefully at the wrist and closes
with a sparkling bezeled rivoli.**

► 1. Base

Mix the size 8° beads, matte purple and metallic purple size 11° beads, triangle beads, bicone crystals, and fire-polished beads into a pile. Pick up 4 size 8° beads to create the first right angle weave unit. Continue working in right angle weave, changing bead types every few units, until you have a row of units 2 inches (5.1 cm) wide (figure 1).

Note: You'll find the result more soothing to the eye if you work in patches of color with the occasional bicone crystal or fire-polished bead to catch the light. Also, to keep the base flat, work 2 size 11° beads in place of 1 size 8° bead, bicone crystal, or fire-polished bead. Treat the 2 size 11° beads as 1 bead, passing through both to create 1 right angle weave unit edge.

Work subsequent rows of freeform right angle weave, introducing the occasional bicone crystal or fire-polished bead into your weave, until the base is 1 inch (2.5 cm) longer than your wrist measurement.

► 2. Gather

Weave through the beadwork to exit down through a bead along the top edge of the base, 1 inch (2.5 cm) from the end. Pass down through each adjacent bead in that row. Pull snug to gather the fabric (figure 2). Weave in the thread and trim. Start a new thread that exits 1 inch (2.5 cm) from the other end of the base and repeat the gather.

► 3. Bezel

Row 1: Use bronze size 15° beads to work a row of right angle weave 27 units long (or long enough to fit around the rivoli). To make sure the strip will fit, wrap the row along the edge of the rivoli; if there is a 1- or 2-bead space, the strip is the correct size. The final unit count should be an odd number.

Rows 2–4: Use bronze size 15° beads to work right angle weave, creating a strip 27 units wide and 4 rows long.

Ring: Join the short ends together (see figure 20 in Fundamentals, page 23) to form a ring. Weave through the beads to exit a row 1 edge bead.

Shaping: Without adding beads, weave through the row 1 edge beads and pull tight to form the ring into a cup-shaped bezel. Place the rivoli, face up, into the cup. Weave through beads to exit from a row 4 edge bead. Weave through the row 4 edge beads and pull tight, cupping the beads around the rivoli. If thread shows, add 1 size 15° or 11° bead between every 2 beads in the round.

Embellishment: Weave through the beads to exit from a row 3 bead whose hole is horizontal to the edge of the rivoli. Add 1 amethyst size 15° bead and pass through the next horizontal bead (figure 3). Repeat around. Weave through the beadwork to exit from a row 2 horizontal bead; add 1 amethyst size 11° bead between each horizontal bead.

► 4. Assembly

Rivoli: Center the rivoli on one of the gathered ends of the base. Sew the bottom of the bezel to the base by exiting a bead on the bezel and passing through an adjacent base bead (figure 4). Weave in the thread and trim.

Clasp: Start a new thread that exits from the base, underneath the rivoli. Securely sew the tab side of the closure to the base. Start a new thread that exits from the top side of the base, opposite the rivoli. Securely sew the bar side of the closure to the base (figure 5).

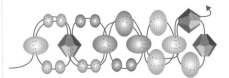

figure 1

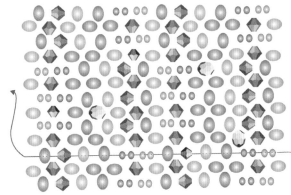

figure 2

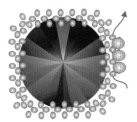

figure 3

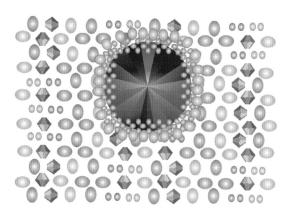

figure 4

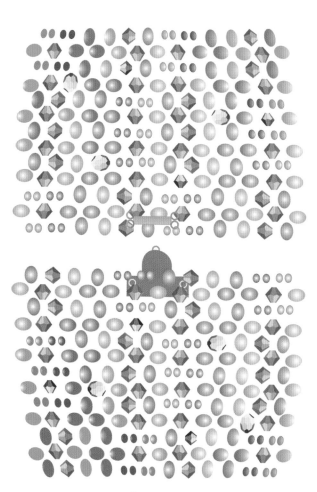

figure 5

CHAPTER FOUR
ROPES

SHIMMER QUEEN

This tubular necklace has both the strength and the visual heft to support a magnificent lampworked focal bead. Fire-polished beads give it shine, while metallic seed beads create spots of color.

The necklace closes with a magnetic clasp.

SUPPLIES

Basic Beading Kit (page 10)

Metallic gold AB size 11° seed beads, 15 g

Metallic aqua size 15° seed beads, 4 g

400 light rose AB fire-polished beads, 3 mm

1 gold magnetic clasp, 9 mm

1 blue, gold, and purple lampworked focal bead with a 7/8-inch (11 mm) hole, 37 x 28 mm

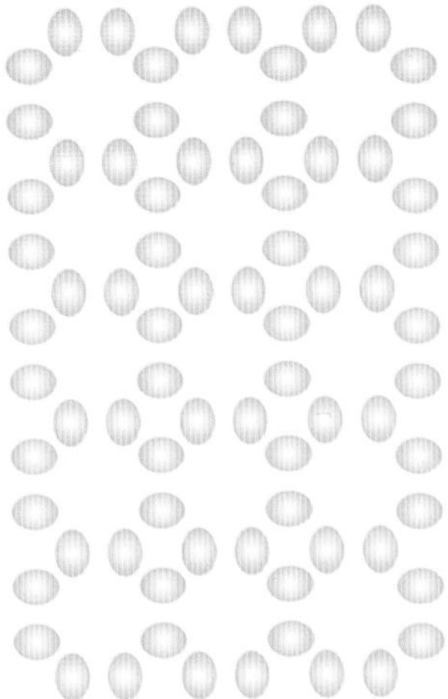

figure 1

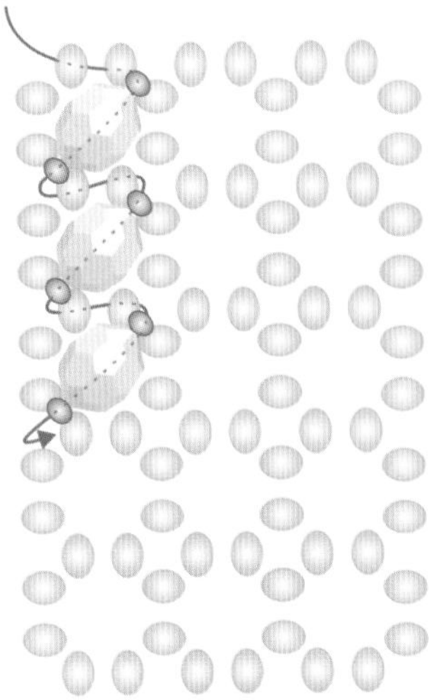

figure 2

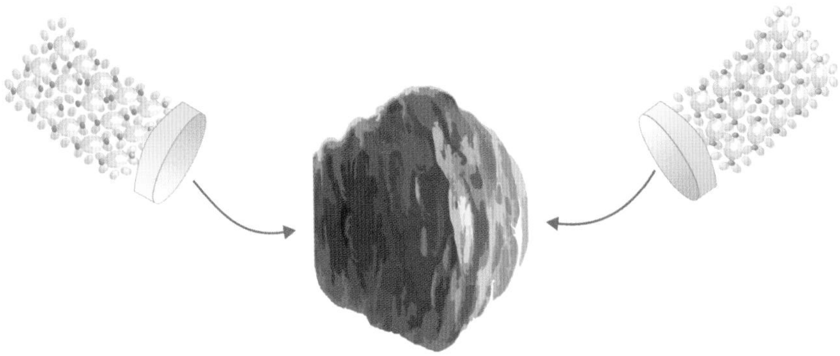

figure 3

▶ 1. Rope

Use size 11° seed beads, 2 beads on each side, to stitch a length of right angle weave 3 units wide by 100 rows, or 19 inches (48.3 cm) long (figure 1).

Join the long ends using 2 size 11° seed beads to make a rope (see figure 20 in Fundamentals, page 23).

▶ 2. Embellishment

Orient the rope vertically. Weave through the beads to exit from 2 top size 11° seed beads from left to right. Pick up 1 size 15° bead, 1 fire-polished bead, and 1 size 15° bead. Pass through the next 2 size 11° bottom beads from left to right. Repeat for the entire length of the rope on all 4 columns (figure 2). Secure the thread and trim.

▶ 3. Clasp

Attach one side of the clasp to the end of the rope by threading one needle, doubling the thread, and then passing the two ends through another needle. Wrap the thread several times around the shank of the clasp. Insert the two needles into the body of the rope, exiting to the outside of the beadwork on opposite sides. Weave through several adjacent beads, weave in the threads, and trim. Repeat on the other side.

Slip the lampworked bead onto the beaded rope. Press the clasp together and allow the lampworked bead to slide over it to hide the closure (figure 3).

41

SUPPLIES

Basic Beading Kit (page 10)

Green size 15° seed beads, < 0.5 g

Green size 11° seed beads, < 0.5 g

8 turquoise AB2X bicone crystal beads, 3 mm

2 olivine cubic zirconia horizontally drilled faceted teardrop beads, 9 x 36 mm

2 gold-filled ear wires

MEDICI DROP

Beaded diamonds and cubic zirconia drops evoke the jewels that might have adorned the noblewomen of the Renaissance.

figure 1

▶ 1. Unit 1

Pick up 3 size 15° beads and 1 size 11° bead 4 times. Tie an overhand knot to form a tight circle. Pass through the first 3 size 15° beads and 1 size 11° bead. Pick up 1 size 15° bead and pass through the next size 11° bead, pulling tight. Repeat 3 more times to form a square (figure 1). Weave through the beads to exit from a corner size 15° bead on the bottom of the square.

Continued on next page

▶ 2. Unit 2

Pick up 2 size 15° beads. Pick up 1 size 11° bead and 5 size 15° beads 3 times. Pick up 1 size 11° bead and 2 size 15° beads. Pass through the corner size 15° bead you last exited from unit 1, the first 2 size 15° beads added in this unit, and the next size 11° bead. Pick up 1 bicone crystal and pass through the next size 11° bead. Repeat 3 more times.

▶ 3. Drop

Pass through the first bicone crystal, the next size 11° bead, and 3 size 15° beads to exit from the bottom corner of the second unit. Pick up 3 size 15° beads and 1 teardrop bead. Pick up 3 size 15° beads and pass through the corner size 15° bead you last exited from unit 2.

▶ 4. Loop

Weave through the beadwork to exit from the corner size 15° bead at the top of unit 1. Pick up 7 size 15° beads and pass through the corner size 15° bead to form a loop (figure 2). Repeat the thread path to reinforce. Weave in the thread and trim. Add an ear wire to the loop of seven beads.

Repeat to make the second earring.

figure 2

43

SUPPLIES

Basic Beading Kit (page 10)

Smoke 6-pound braided beading thread

290 green round crystal pearl beads, 4 mm

Matte forest iris size 15° seed beads, 5 g

Matte forest iris size 11° seed beads, 2 g

128 olivine AB bicone crystal beads, 3 mm

144 crystal AB round crystal beads, 2 mm

24 green round crystal pearl beads, 3 mm

30 green round crystal pearl beads, 6 mm to 12 mm

1 olivine AB margarita crystal bead, 8 mm

1 black sewing snap, ¹⁄₄ inch (6 mm)

CASSIOPEIA

This choker closes with an embellished clasp that hides a fastening snap. It can be worn alone or with the luscious spray of pearls that forms the pendant.

figure 1

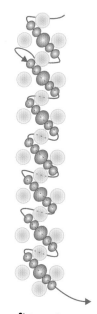

figure 2

▶ 1. Strap

Use 4-mm pearls to create a strap of right angle weave 1 unit wide by 75 units long for a 19-inch (48.3 cm) choker (figure 1).

Orient the strap so the end points up. Exit from the top horizontal-hole pearl bead, from right to left. Pick up 2 size 15° beads, 1 size 11° bead, and 2 size 15° beads. Pass through the horizontal-hole pearl bead directly below the one last exited, from right to left, so the seed beads lie diagonally across the 4-pearl unit. Repeat down the length of the strip (figure 2).

Continued on next page

Clasp medallion

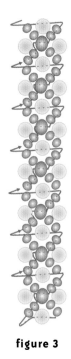

figure 3

figure 4

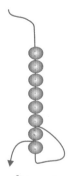

figure 5

figure 6

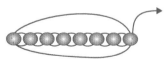

figure 7

figure 8

Pick up 2 size 15° beads and pass through the size 11° bead placed in the center of the last unit embellished. Pick up 2 more size 15° beads and pass through the horizontal-hole pearl bead above the one you last exited, from right to left. Continue for the length of the strap (figure 3). Turn the strap over and repeat this step so both sides of the strap have crisscrosses down the center.

Orient the strap so the end points up. Weave through the beads to exit down through a side bead in the last unit. Pick up one 3-mm bicone crystal and pass down through the side bead of the next unit. Repeat along one strap edge. Repeat for the other edge, this time using 2-mm round crystal beads. Be careful not to pull too tight (figure 4). Weave in the thread and trim. Set aside.

▶ 2. Clasp Medallion

Start the clasp medallion by working an 8-bead ladder-stitched strip: Pick up 8 size 11° beads and pass through the second-to-last bead just strung (figure 5).

Pass through the next-to-last bead strung and pull tight (figure 6). Repeat until all beads are aligned, side by side.

Orient the strip so the working thread exits from the top of the last bead. Pass through the top of the first bead and the bottom of the last bead to create a ring (figures 7 and 8). Orient the beads so the holes point outward; exit toward the outside of the ring.

Pick up 3 size 11° beads. Pass down through the next ladder-stitched bead and up through the following one. Repeat around the ring to make a total of 4 picots. Weave through the beads to exit from the first bead added in the first picot (figure 9).

Pick up 5 size 11° beads and pass down through the third bead of the first picot; don't pass through a bead on the ladder-stitched ring. Pick up a 4-mm pearl bead and pass up through the first bead of the second picot. Repeat this step 2 times for a total of 3 picots and 3 pearls. Pick up 5 size 11° beads and pass down through the third bead of the fourth picot. Pass through the bead pearl at one end of the strap, up through the 3 beads of the first picot, and down through the adjacent ladder-stitched bead. Pass through the ladder-stitched bead to the right, exiting toward the point (figure 10).

figure 9

Pick up a 3-mm pearl bead and a 3-mm bicone crystal. Pass through the middle bead of the first 5-bead picot added in the previous step. Pick up 3 size 11° beads and pass through the size 11° you last exited again to form a loop. Working counter-clockwise, pick up a 3-mm bicone crystal and a 3mm pearl, then pass down through the next ladder-stitched bead on the ring and up through the following one. Continue until you have embellished all 4 picots (figure 11). Pick up the margarita bead and 1 size 15° bead. Pass back through the margarita and the ladder-stitched bead opposite the one you last exited. Repeat the thread path to reinforce.

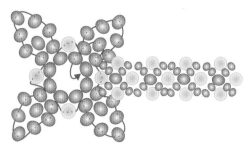

figure 10

Securely stitch one half of the snap to the back of the medallion (figure 12). Weave in the thread and trim.

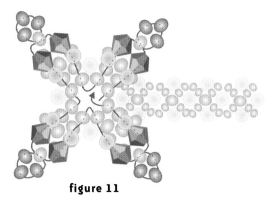

figure 11

Continued on next page

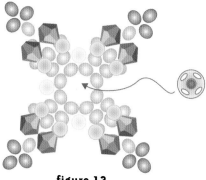

figure 12

▶ 3. Clasp Tab

Start a new thread that exits from the pearl bead at the other end of the other strap. Pick up 19 size 11° beads and pass back through the fourth bead added. Pick up 3 more size 11° beads and pass through the end pearl bead from the opposite side (figure 13).

Pass through the first 6 seed beads added, pick up 1 size 11° bead, skip 3 seed beads, and pass through the tenth seed bead. Continue picking up 1 size 11° bead, skipping 3 seed beads, and entering the next one until you've added 4 seed beads in all (figure 14).

Securely stitch the other snap half to the tab's face (figure 15). Weave in the thread and trim. Set aside.

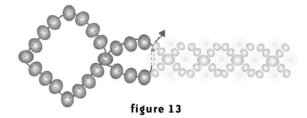

figure 13

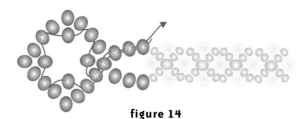

figure 14

figure 15

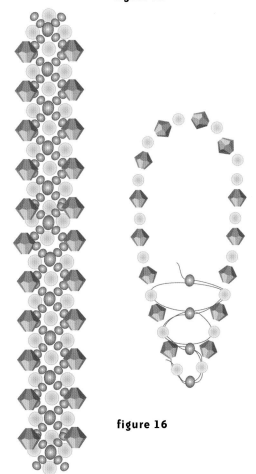

figure 16

▶ **4. Pendant**

Repeat step 1 to make a strap 14 rows long, but use 3-mm bicone crystals to embellish both edges. Fold the strap in half. Join the bottom 3 units along the sides using size 11° beads (figure 16; also see figure 20 in Fundamentals, page 23).

Exit from a size 11° bead on the front of the strap and pick up 12 to 15 assorted pearls, 2-mm round crystal beads, and 3-mm bicone crystal beads, ending with a 2-mm round crystal bead. Skip the last bead strung, pass back through the rest of the beads just added, and weave back into the strap beads (figure 17). Repeat down the folded strap's front to make a total of 16 fringes, randomly varying the sizes and lengths of the embellishments as you go. Weave in the thread and trim. Slip the completed pendant over the strap.

figure 17

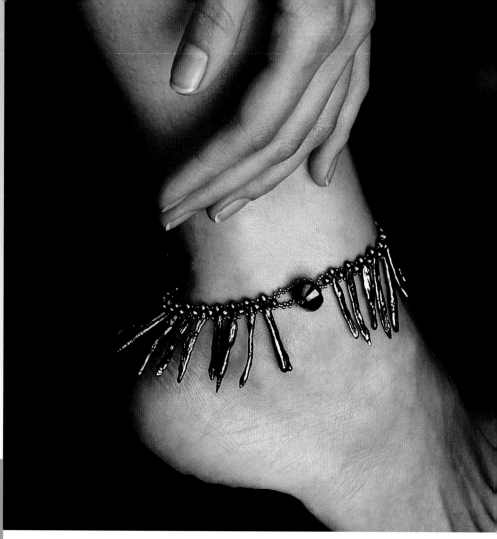

SUPPLIES

Basic Beading Kit (page 10)

65 brown freshwater pearl round beads, 3 mm

Bronze size 15° seed beads, < 1 g

32 brown freshwater pearl top-drilled stick beads, between 23 mm and 37 mm long

1 brown iris Czech rivoli with vertical hole, 14 x 9 mm

KA'IULANI

Warm brown pearls and irregular stick pearls come together to create a graceful anklet. Just add skimpy sandals and tropical weather and you have a winning design.

▶ 1. Base

Pick up 1 round pearl, 1 seed bead, 1 stick pearl, 1 seed bead, 1 round pearl, 1 seed bead, 1 round pearl, and 1 seed bead. Leave an 8-inch (20.3 cm) tail as you tie a knot to form a tight circle. Orient the work so that the first round pearl faces right and the stick pearl is on the bottom. Pass the working thread through the first pearl added (figure 1).

Pick up 1 seed bead, 1 stick pearl, 1 seed bead, 1 round pearl, 1 seed bead, 1 round

pearl, and 1 seed bead. Working counterclockwise, pass through the side pearl from the first unit, and continue though the seed bead, the stick pearl, the next seed bead, and the new side pearl (figure 2).

Measure your ankle directly above the ankle bone. Continue adding units to the base until you reach this length. (The anklet shown uses 32 units for a 9½-inch [24.1 cm]-long piece.) Weave through the beads to exit from the last side pearl.

▶ 2. Clasp

Pick up 34 seed beads. Pass through the side pearl again to form a loop.

Pick up 1 seed bead, skip 1 seed bead on the loop, and pass through the seed bead. Repeat around the loop to add a total of 17 seed beads (figure 3). Pass through the side pearl, weave in the working thread, and trim.

Place a needle on the tail thread and weave through the beads to exit from the first side pearl at that end of the base. Pick up 6 seed beads, the rivoli bead, and 3 seed beads and pass back through the rivoli bead. Pick up 6 seed beads and pass through the side pearl bead. Repeat the thread path to reinforce. Weave in the thread and trim (figure 4).

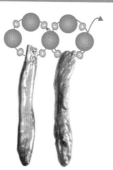

figure 2

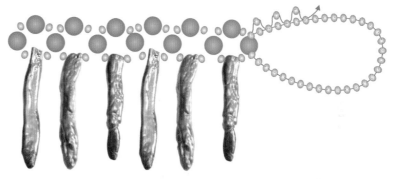

figure 3

figure 1

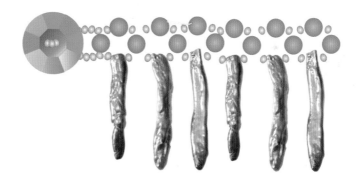

figure 4

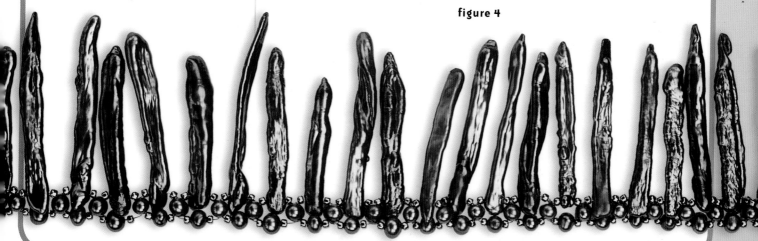

CHAPTER FIVE
ARMATURES

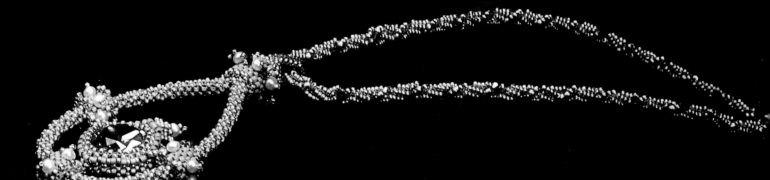

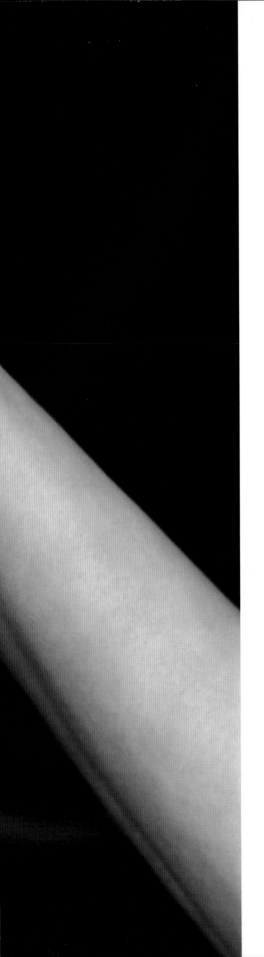

BEADED
BANGLE

A beaded length of right angle weave is joined over an armature of rubber to create a classic bangle. Its wonderful texture comes from using two sizes of beads. Make five or six of these and wear them all at once for a look of playful sophistication.

SUPPLIES

Basic Beading Kit (page 10)

Flexible tape measure

Rubber cord for armature, 0.188-inch (4.8 mm) diameter, 7 to 10 inches (17.8 cm to 25.4 cm) long

Utility scissors

3/8-inch (9 mm) heat-shrink tubing, 1 inch (2.5 cm)

Hair dryer or heat gun

Smoke 6-pound braided beading thread

Bronze size 11° seed beads, 10 g

Purple green matte size 8° seed beads, 20 g

Contrasting-color thread or correction fluid (optional)

▶ 1. Base Ring

Determine the length needed for the rubber armature by holding your thumb across your palm as if you were putting on a bangle and measuring your hand around the widest part, near the base of your thumb. Add 1 inch (2.5 cm) to this measurement and cut the rubber cord so the ends are flush.

Insert the 2 rubber ends into the heat-shrink tubing. Push the rubber on each side so the ends securely butt against one another within the tubing. Hold the rubber and tubing together as you use the hair dryer or heat gun to shrink the tubing down onto the rubber (figure 1). This may take a few minutes. Set the base ring aside.

figure 1

Continue rows to desired length.

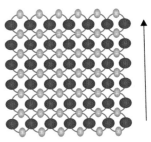

figure 2

▶ 2. Strip

Use doubled thread to work a strip of right angle weave 6 units wide and 2 inches (5.1 cm) longer than your hand measurement. (The bangle shown is 65 units long, or 10 inches [25.4 cm].) Use size 11° beads on the top and bottom of each unit and size 8° beads on the side (figure 2). Don't cut the thread.

Mark an edge bead on the same side of the first and last rows to ensure that when you join the short ends you won't twist the beadwork. One way to do this is to tie a small piece of contrasting thread around the bead; or you can apply a removable substance such as correcting fluid.

▶ 3. Join

Lay the beadwork underneath the base ring and bring the long edges together on top (figure 3). Starting with row 1, begin to join the long edges by using size 11° top and bottom beads to connect the size 8° side beads (see figure 20 in Fundamentals, page 23).

When you're 2 inches (5.1 cm) from the end, lay the remainder of the strip on the base ring to determine whether you've made enough rows to cover it. If not, right angle weave additional rows in the beadwork. If the beadwork is too long, remove rows. Complete the join.

Position the 2 marked beads opposite one another. Join the short ends of the strip by adding size 8° beads (figure 4; also see figure 20 in Fundamentals, page 23). Weave in the thread and trim.

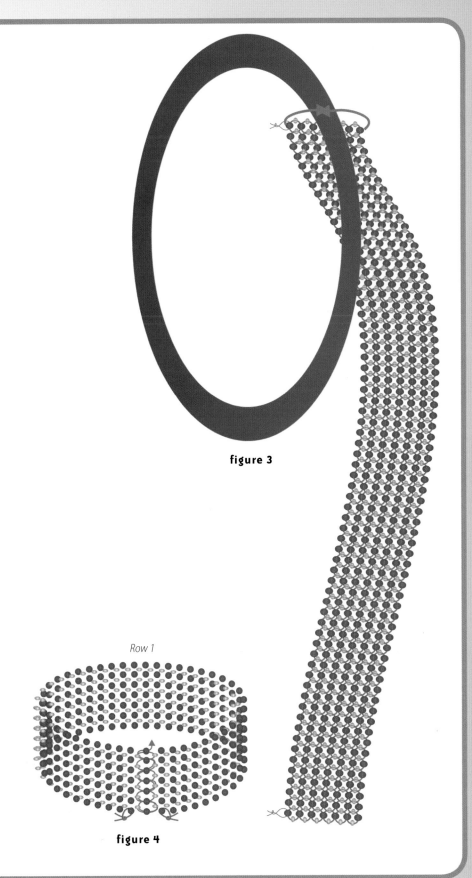

figure 3

Row 1

figure 4

FLEUR FANTAISIE

A simple necklace is a great way to showcase a favorite focal bead. The whimsical lampworked bead in this version reminds me of the fanciful costumes worn for Cirque du Soleil performances. It was made by one of my favorite glass artists, Gail Crosman Moore.

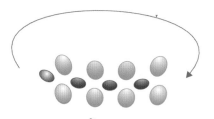

figure 1

▶ 1. Rope

Work a rope of tubular right angle weave that's 4 units around and 24 inches (61 cm) long. Use matte blue size 11° beads for the sides of each unit and size 8° beads for the tops and bottoms (figure 1; also see figures 17 and 18 in Fundamentals, page 22). Set the rope aside.

▶ 2. Armature

Use round-nose pliers to form a ¼-inch (6 mm) flat loop ⁵⁄₁₆ inch (8 mm) from one end of the copper wire. Carefully insert the wire into the right angle weave rope, straight end first, until it extends 1 inch (2.5 cm) from the other end. Bend another ¼-inch (6 mm) flat loop on this end of the wire. This leaves 4 inches (10.2 cm) of the rope empty at one end.

Continued on next page

Continued on next page

SUPPLIES

Basic Beading Kit (page 10)

Size 11° seed beads:
   Matte blue, 5 g
   Metallic blue, 0.5 g

Peach AB size 8° seed beads, 15 g

14-gauge copper wire, 19 inches (48.3 cm) long

Dark metallic red size 15° seed beads, 0.5 g

1 violet AB center-drilled teardrop crystal, 6 x 9 mm

1 jet AB2X bicone crystal bead, 3 mm

1 raku-style lampworked cone blossom pendant with loop, 29 x 45 mm

Round-nose pliers

Dowels:
   ³⁄₁₆ inch (4 mm) in diameter, 6 inches (15.2 cm) or longer

   ¼ inch (6 mm) in diameter, 6 inches (15.2 cm) or longer

Measure 5 inches (12.7 cm) up the wire from the exposed end. Loosely wrap the beaded wire around the ³⁄₁₆-inch (4 mm) dowel one and a half times. Bend the rest of the beaded wire into a circle with a diameter of 6 inches (15.2 cm) to fit around your neck. Set aside.

▶ 3. Beaded Bead

Use matte blue size 11° beads to work a strip of right angle weave 7 units wide and 7 rows high. Join to create a tube (see figure 20 in Fundamentals, page 23). Weave through the beads to exit from a horizontal bead in row 1.

Slide the tube onto the ¼-inch (6 mm) dowel and orient it vertically. Starting at the top, embellish the tube. See figure 2 for bead types as you complete the following rounds:

Round 1: Pick up 5 size 8° beads and pass through the next horizontal bead. Repeat 7 more times. Pass through a vertical bead between rows and a horizontal bead in round 2.

Round 2: Pick up 5 size 11° beads and pass through the next horizontal bead. Repeat 7 times and pass through beads to round 3.

Round 3: Pick up 1 size 8° bead and 1 size 15° bead. Pass back through the size 8° bead and into the next horizontal bead. Repeat 7 times and pass through beads to round 4.

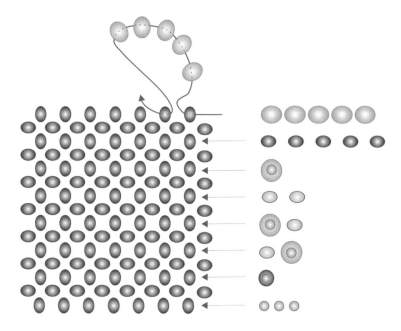

figure 2

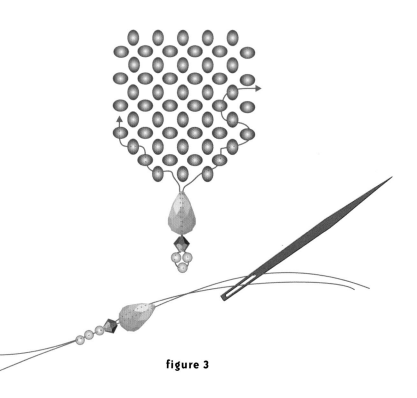

figure 3

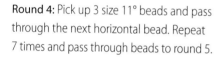

figure 4

Round 4: Pick up 3 size 11° beads and pass through the next horizontal bead. Repeat 7 times and pass through beads to round 5.

Round 5: Pick up 1 size 8° bead and 1 size 15° bead. Pass back through the size 8° bead and into the next horizontal bead. Pick up 1 size 11° bead and pass through the next horizontal bead. Continue to alternate between the size 8° bead fringe and size 11° beads until you have completed the row. Pass through beads to round 6.

Round 6: Repeat round 5 but alternate the order in which you place the size 11° and size 8° beads.

Round 7: Pick up 1 size 11° bead and 1 size 15° bead. Pass back through the size 11° bead and into the next horizontal bead. Repeat 7 times and pass through beads to round 8.

Round 8: Pick up 3 size 15° beads and pass through the next horizontal bead. Repeat 7 times. Remove the dowel. Weave in the thread and trim.

Pass 3 feet (0.9 m) of thread through the needle and pull the ends even. Pass both thread ends through a second needle. Pick up the teardrop crystal, the bicone crystal, and 3 size 15° beads. Pass one needle back through the bicone crystal and teardrop crystal to make a dangle. Weave each needle through the last round of the beaded bead's tube on opposite sides. This will center the dangle at the bottom of the beaded bead, as shown in figure 3, where the beaded bead is shown unembellished for clarity. Weave in one of the working threads and trim.

▶ **4. Assembly**

Attach the lampworked bead to the end of the rope by threading 1 needle, doubling the thread, and then passing the 2 ends through another needle. Wrap the thread several times around the loop of the bead. Insert the 2 needles into the body of the rope, exiting to the outside of the bead-work on opposite sides. Weave through several adjacent beads, weave in the threads and trim. If the focal bead doesn't have a loop, use a head pin and form a wrapped loop to hang the bead.

Slide the beaded bead on the exposed wire. Securely stitch the beaded bead to the rope (figure 4).

ETRUSCAN TREASURE

A crystal rivoli mounted in a graceful beaded teardrop takes center stage.

Glints of crystal in the cord set off a necklace worthy of ancient queens.

SUPPLIES FOR PENDANT

Basic Beading Kit (page 10)

Gold 16-gauge metal wire, 7 inches (17.8 cm)

Smoke 6-pound braided beading thread

Size 15° seed beads:
   Metallic gold, 5 g (A)
   Metallic blue matte, < 0.5 g (B)

Size 11° cylinder beads:
   Gold matte, 2 g (C)
   Metallic gold AB, < 1 g (D)

24 white freshwater pearls, 3 mm

5 Montana blue AB bicone crystal beads, 3 mm

1 dark indigo round crystal rivoli, 18 or 20 mm

2 vermeil star spacers, 6 mm

1 vermeil daisy spacer, 5 mm

Flat-nose pliers

Wire cutters

SUPPLIES FOR NECKLACE
(for 18 inches [45.7cm])

Basic Beading Kit (page 10)

Smoke 6-pound braided beading thread

Metallic gold size 15° seed beads, 5 g (same as A)

Metallic gold size 11° seed beads, 2 g (E)

28 Montana blue AB bicone crystal beads, 3 mm

1 gold toggle bar, 29 mm

figure 1

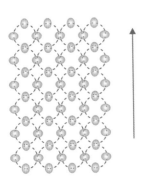

figure 2

figure 3

figure 4

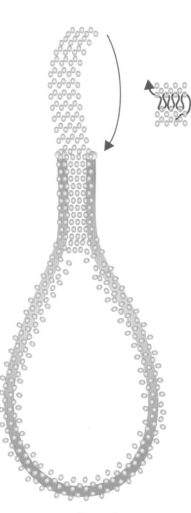

figure 5

▶ **1. Armature**

Use your fingers to bend the wire into the approximate shape shown in figure 1. Define the shape by using flat-nose pliers to make 90-degree bends at the neck, leaving ¾-inch (1.9 cm) wire stems on each side (figure 1). Set the wire aside.

Use A beads to create a strip of right angle weave 4 units wide and 6½ inches (16.5 cm) long (figure 2). Don't cut the thread.

Wrap the strip around the wire, right beneath the bends, so the long ends of the beadwork touch. Starting at row 1, add A beads in the top and bottom positions of each unit to join the beadwork into a tube around the wire (figure 3; also see figure 20 in Fundamentals, page 23). Lengthen or shorten the beadwork as required to fit the curve in the wire.

▶ **2. Bail**

Weave through the beadwork to exit from an edge bead at one end of the tube. Pick up 1 A bead and pass through the next edge bead. Repeat 2 more times to work peyote stitch around the tube. Pick up 1 A bead and pass through an edge bead at the other end of the tube. Work peyote stitch around this end of the tube, adding 3 beads (figure 4). Pick up 1 A bead and pass through the adjacent right angle weave bead at the first tube end and the first peyote-stitched bead to step up for the next round.

Use A beads to work tubular peyote stitch around both wires for 12 rounds, adding 8 beads in each round. When you encounter the bead between the wires, treat it as an "up" bead and pass through it after adding a bead. Pass through the first bead of the previous and current rounds to step up for

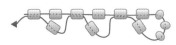

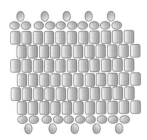

figure 6

figure 7

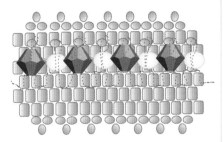

figure 8

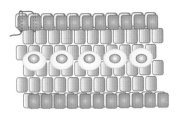

figure 9

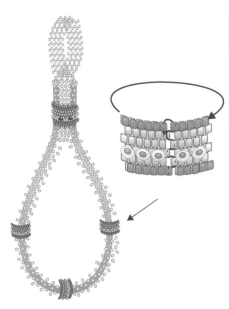

figure 10

each round. Use wire cutters to trim the wire flush or a little below the beadwork.

Work flat peyote stitch off the front 3 spaces of the peyote-stitched tube to make a strip 30 rows long. Stitch the last row to the other side of the tube to create the pendant's bail (figure 5). Weave in the thread and trim.

▶ 3. Bail Embellishment

Use C beads to work a strip of peyote stitch 6 beads wide and 32 rows long. In every third and fourth row, pick up 3 A beads, then add the first C bead for the row to create an edge design (figure 6 and figure 7).

Weave through the beadwork to exit from a C bead in the center of the strip. Pick up 1 pearl and 1 A bead. Pass back through the pearl and the adjacent C bead down the strip. Pick up one 3-mm crystal bead

and 1 A bead. Pass back through the crystal and the adjacent C bead down the strip. Repeat, alternating pearls and crystals down the center of the strip to add a total of 5 pearls and 5 crystals (figure 8).

Stitch the first and last rows of the strip together to form a tube. Slide the tube over the bail. **Note:** The tube will stay in place once you pass the necklace through the bail.

▶ 4. Bands

Use C beads to work a band of peyote stitch 6 beads wide and 22 rows long. Weave through the beads to exit from a C bead in the center of the band. Pick up 1 pearl and 1 A bead and pass back through the pearl. Weave through the beads to exit from a C bead 2 beads down the band from the place you last exited. Repeat to add a total of 5 pearls.

Weave through the beads to exit out from an edge C bead. Pick up 1 D bead and pass through the C bead last exited and the next edge C bead, allowing the D bead to sit on the front of the beadwork. Repeat to add 1 D bead to each C bead on both edges (figure 9).

Wrap the band around the center bottom of the armature as shown in figure 10. Stitch the first and last rows together to form a tube, placing the join on the inside edge of the armature. Stitch the band to the armature to secure it in place. Weave in the thread and trim.

Repeat this step to make 2 more bands, positioning them on the sides of the armature as shown in figure 10.

Continued on next page

figure 11

▶ 5. Bezel

Use A beads to make a strip of right angle weave wide enough to fit around the edge of the rivoli. Use an odd number of units so that, when joined, you have an even number of spaces. Test the size. The strip should fit around the edge of the rivoli with only a slight space between each end. Make your strip 4 rows long. Join the short ends together (see figure 20 in Fundamentals, page 23).

Exiting from an edge bead, weave through the last round's edge beads without adding beads between, and pull tight. This will form the ring into a cup-shaped bezel. Hold the cup with the round you just pulled tight on the bottom and place the rivoli into the cup, right side up.

Weave through the beads to exit an edge bead on top of the rivoli. Pass through

each bead in this round as you did for the back of the bezel. If the thread shows, you may need to add 1 A bead between every 2 beads in the round. Weave through the beadwork to exit from a bead whose hole is horizontal to the edge of the rivoli, 1 row back from the front edge.

Pick up 1 C bead and pass through the next horizontal-hole A bead in the round. Repeat to add a round of embellishment beads. Weave through the beadwork to exit from the bottom A bead of the next round; repeat to add 1 C bead between each horizontal A bead. Add 1 B bead between each C bead just placed. Weave through the beads to exit from a C bead from the first round of embellishment.

▶ 6. Assembly

Position the bezel between the 3 bands on the armature. Use your fingers to gently bend the armature to create a 3-mm space

at each of the 3 attachment points.

Use the working thread on the bezel (which should be exiting a C bead) to pick up 1 A bead and 1 pearl. Pass through a C bead on the inside midpoint of the right-hand armature band, where there's no pearl embellishment. Weave through 2 or 3 adjacent C beads and exit from the original C bead you entered on the band. Pass back through the pearl and the C bead last exited on the rivoli. Repeat the thread path to reinforce. Weave through the bezel beads to reach the bottom rivoli/band attachment point. Repeat this step to connect the armature's bottom and side attachment points.

Weave through the beads to exit from an A bead at the top of the rivoli. Pick up two 6-mm spacers, the 5-mm spacer, 1 pearl, and 3 A beads. Pass back through the pearl and spacers and the next A bead on the rivoli to make a fringe (figure 11). Weave in

figure 12

figure 13

figure 14

figure 15

<... >

the thread and trim. Set the pendant aside.

▶ 7. Necklace

Use doubled thread to pick up 4 E beads (hereafter called core beads) and 4 A beads (which we'll call spiral beads), leaving an 8-inch (20.3 cm) tail. Pass through the core beads again and push the spiral beads to the side (figure 12).

Pick up 1 core bead and 4 spiral beads. Pass through the last 3 core beads and the new core bead. Push the spiral beads to

the side (figure 13).

Repeat this step to your desired length, except on every twelfth repeat use one 3-mm crystal as your core bead and 5 A beads as your spiral beads. Pass through the previous 3 core beads and the crystal. Push the spiral beads to the side (figure 14).

Pick up 12 A beads. Pass through the toggle bar's loop and back through the third, second, and first A bead just strung.

Repeat the thread path to reinforce. Weave in the thread and trim.

Use the tail thread to pick up enough E beads to make a loop that the toggle bar can easily pass through. Pass back through the beads at the end of the cord. Weave through the beads to exit from the first E bead of the loop. Use A beads to work peyote stitch around the loop, using 3 beads in each stitch (figure 15). Weave in the thread and trim.

RINGLETS

Inspired by the color and patterns of Heather Trimlett's lampworked rings, this necklace design features seed bead rings woven over aluminum armatures. Pairing the ringlets with matte silver chain and Heather's lampwork gives the piece an utterly hip look.

SUPPLIES

Basic Beading Kit (page 10)

Size 15° seed beads:
  Yellow, 0.5 g
  Orange, 0.5 g
  Black, 0.5 g
  White, 0.5 g
  Silver, 0.5 g

Anodized aluminum rings:

  1 fuchsia, 3 mm thick, 1¼ inches (3.2 cm) in diameter

  1 silver, 2 mm thick, ¾ inch (1.9 cm) in diameter

  2 silver, 3 mm thick, 1 inch (2.5 cm) in diameter

  1 fuchsia, 3 mm thick, 1 inch (2.5 cm) in diameter

Size 11° seed beads:
  White, 0.5 g
  Matte black, 0.5 g

20 matte black size 8° seed beads

30-mm silver chain with varied-size links, 30 inches (76.2 cm) long

1 black and white lampworked glass ring, 40 mm in diameter

1 black, white, orange, and yellow lampworked glass ring, 30 mm in diameter

1 black, white, and clear lampworked glass ring, 22 mm in diameter

Wire cutters

2 pair of chain-nose pliers

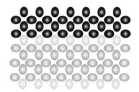

figure 1

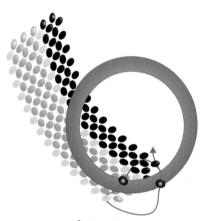

figure 2

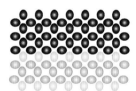

figure 3

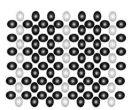

figure 4

▶ 1. Ring One

Use size 15° beads to work a strip of right angle weave 39 units wide and 5 rows high in the following color pattern:

Row 1: Yellow bottoms; orange sides and tops (figure 1).

Row 2: Orange sides and tops.

Row 3: Orange sides, yellow tops.

Row 4: Black sides and tops.

Row 5: Black sides and tops.

Note: The number of units given here is what worked for me. However, the slight variance in the size of beads, the type of thread, and your particular tension may change the count. To measure, wrap the first row of right angle weave around the circumference of the aluminum ring you're working with. There should be a 1- or 2-bead space between the two ends. You'll generally want an even number of spaces to allow for embellishing every other space differently. If you start with an odd number of units, once you complete the join you'll have an even number of spaces.

Join the short edges to make a ring, using corresponding colors in each row as you insert the size 15° join beads (see figure 20 in Fundamentals, page 23). Weave through adjacent beads to an edge bead.

Position the beaded ring inside the 1¼-inch (3.2 cm) aluminum ring. Fold the beadwork over the aluminum ring, bringing the long ends together on the outside edge. Join the long edges using black size 15° beads (figure 2; also see figure 20 in Fundamentals, page 23). Weave in the thread and trim. Set aside. ***Note:*** At first, the beaded ring may appear too large to fit. But as you continue to join the outside edge, the beads will move together and fit inside the ring perfectly.

▶ 2. Ring Two

Use yellow, orange, and black size 15° beads to work a strip of right angle weave 29 units wide and 4 rows high following the pattern in figure 3.

Join the short edges to make a ring, using corresponding beads to make the join. Weave through the beadwork to an edge bead. Position the beaded ring inside the ¾-inch (1.9 cm) aluminum ring. Join the beaded ring's long ends using yellow size 15° beads. Weave in the thread and trim. Set aside.

▶ 3. Ring Three

Use black and white size 15° beads to work a strip of right angle weave 32 units long and 6 rows high following the pattern in figure 4.

Join the short edges to make a ring, using black size 15° beads. Weave through the beads to an edge bead. Position the ring inside a silver 1-inch (2.5 cm) aluminum ring. Join the long ends using black size 15° beads. Weave in the thread and trim. Set aside.

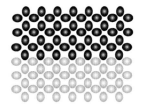

figure 5

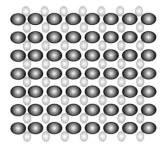

figure 6

Rings of Saturn includes rings formed over an armature, like those in *Ringlets*. They revolve around a shaped peyote core.

▶ 4. Ring Four

Use black and white size 15° beads to work a strip of right angle weave 31 units long and 6 rows high, following the pattern in figure 5.

Join the short edges to make a ring, using the corresponding beads in each row as you insert the size 15° join beads. Weave through the beads to an edge bead. Position the beaded ring inside a silver 1-inch (2.5 cm) aluminum ring. Join the long ends using size 15° white beads.

Embellish the middle row of the white beads by alternating 1 size 11° white bead with fringes made of 1 black size 8° bead and 1 white size 15° turning bead (see figure 21 in Fundamentals, page 24). Weave in the thread and trim. Set aside.

▶ 5. Ring Five

Use silver size 15° beads and black size 11° beads to work a strip of right angle weave 29 units long and 6 rows high following the pattern in figure 6.

Join the short edges to make a ring using silver size 15° beads. Weave through the beads to an edge bead. Position the beaded ring inside the fuchsia 1-inch (2.5 cm) aluminum ring. Join the long ends using black size 11° beads. Weave in the thread and trim. Set aside.

▶ 6. Assembly

Use wire cutters to cut 4½ inches (11.4 cm) of chain. Open a small link by grasping it on each side of the opening with chain-nose pliers, then pushing one end forward and one end back. Attach a ringlet or lamp-worked ring and gently pull the link closed. Repeat to connect all of the ringlets and rings with varying lengths of chain.

CHAPTER SIX
EMBELLISHMENTS

CAPPADOCIA

A simple design translates into a chic wide cuff. The woven base of fire-polished beads is embellished to create angles, showing off maximum sparkle. Slightly larger beads give an elegant flare to the edges. An elaborate medallion provides the focal point while hiding the closure.

Medallion

▶ 1. Base

Work a strip of right angle weave 9 units wide and 41 rows long using 3-mm fire-polished beads with a 4-mm green fire-polished bead on the outside of each edge unit. The finished measurement is 7¾ inches (19.9 cm) long, so add or subtract rows as necessary so the strip fits snugly around your wrist.

Orient the strip so the last row points up. Weave through the beadwork to exit from the top bead of the leftmost unit, toward the center of the strip. Pick up 1 size 15° bead and pass through the top bead of the next unit. Repeat across. Set up for the next row by passing through the 4-mm green fire-polished bead at the edge and the ad-jacent 3-mm fire-polished bead in the next row. Embellish the second row with 1 size 8° bead between each 3-mm fire-polished bead. Repeat down the base, alter-nating the embellishment between 1 row of size 15° beads and 1 row of size 8° beads (figure 1; also see figure 21 in Fundamentals, page 24).

Add 1 size 15° bead between each 4-mm fire-polished bead on both long edges (figure 2).

Sew the clasp loop to the front of the base, along the top of one of the short edges. Stitch the clasp tab along the top of the opposite end, at the back of the beadwork (figure 3).

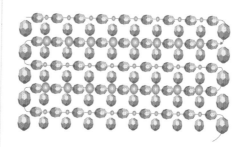

figure 1

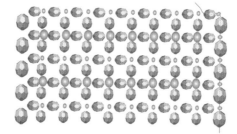

figure 2

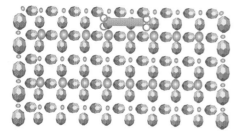

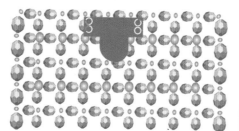

figure 3

Continued on next page

73

SUPPLIES FOR BRACELET

Basic Beading Kit (page 10)

706 green iris fire-polished beads, 3 mm

84 green iris fire-polished beads, 4 mm

Metallic bronze size 15° seed beads, 1.5 g

Metallic bronze size 8° seed beads, 5 g

1 black slide sewing clasp, 18 mm

SUPPLIES FOR MEDALLION

Basic Beading Kit (page 10)

Matte gold AB size 11° seed beads, 0.5 g

16 olivine AB bicone crystal beads, 3 mm

Matte blue size 15° seed beads, 0.2 g

8 indicolite bicone crystal beads, 4 mm

4 bronze fire-polished beads, 4 mm

4 matte blue size 8° seed beads

figure 4

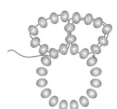

figure 5

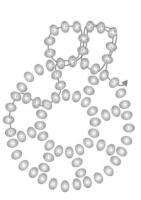

figure 6

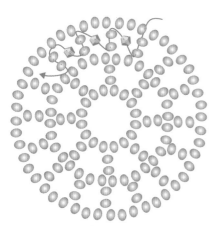

figure 7

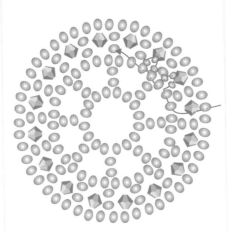

figure 8

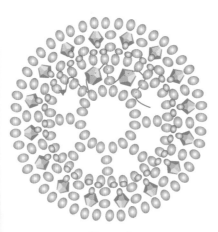

figure 9

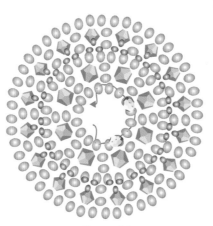

figure 10

▶ **2. Medallion**

Stitch a medallion to use as the bracelet's focal piece and clasp cover.

Base round: Use single thread to pick up 16 size 11° beads. Tie an overhand knot to form a circle (figure 4). Pass through 2 seed beads to the right of the knot.

Round 1: Pick up 8 size 11° beads and pass through the last 2 base beads you exited, making a counterclockwise circle. Pass through the first 2 beads just added (these are your side beads). Pick up 6 size 11° beads, make a clockwise circle, pass back through the next 2 beads on the base, and 2 shared side beads of the first unit, and the 4 top and 2 side beads added in this unit (figure 5). Continue to add 5 more units. Join the seventh and first units with 4 top beads, creating an eighth unit.

Round 2: Use size 11° beads to work 16 units of right angle weave off of round 1; each unit should consist of 2 bottom beads, 2 side beads, and 3 top beads (figure 6). Join the first and last units with 3 top beads. Weave in your thread and trim.

▶ **3. Medallion Embellishment**

Start a doubled thread that exits from 2 side beads in round 2, toward the center. Pick up a 3-mm bicone crystal and pass through the next 2 side beads from top to bottom, toward the center of the medallion. Repeat until you've added a total of 16 crystals (figure 7).

Weave through the beadwork to exit from 2 top beads in round 1. Pick up 3 blue size 15° beads and pass through the next 2 round 1 size 11° beads to form a picot. Repeat to add a total of 16 picots (figure 8).

Pass through beads to exit from 2 side beads in round 1, toward the medallion's edge. Pick up a 4-mm bicone crystal and pass through the next set of side beads from bottom to top. Repeat to add 8 crystals in all (figure 9).

Weave through the beads to exit from 2 seed beads in the base round. Pick up a 4-mm bronze fire-polished bead, skip 2 base round beads, and pass through the next 2 base round beads. Continue until you've added 4 fire-polished beads. Pass through the first 4-mm bronze fire-polished bead added (figure 10).

Pick up 1 blue size 8° bead and pass through the next 4-mm bronze fire-polished bead added to the base round. Repeat to add a total of 4 size 8° beads (figure 11). Pass through all the size 8° and fire-polished beads to reinforce.

Weave through the beadwork to the outside edge of the medallion's round 2. Pass through all the size 11° beads on the outside edge and pull tightly to cup the medallion.

Place the medallion at the end of the base on the opposite side of the clasp tab. Position the medallion so half of its diameter protrudes over the edge. Sew the medallion securely to the base where the two touch (figure 12).

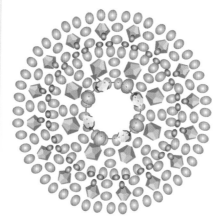

figure 11

figure 12

CASCADE

Graduated lengths of right angle weave create the perfect backdrop to showcase copper-colored crystals and drops.

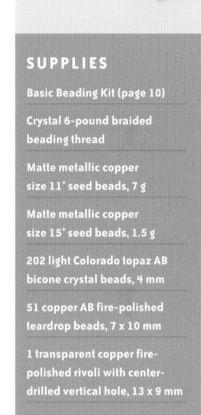

▶ 1. Base

Note: The base is made up of a series of right angle weave columns. The main columns are stitched with 2 size 11° beads per side, and are separated from each other by columns of right angle weave units that are 1 size 11° bead wide and 2 size 11° beads tall. These are called "column separator units" (figure 1).

The individual columns are positioned in groups of 3 called "column groups"; the center column is 1 unit longer than the 2 side ones. The groups of columns are separated by 2 units of right angle weave that are 1 bead wide and 2 beads tall and called "group separator columns."

To begin, use single thread and size 11° beads to weave a strip of right angle weave 2 units wide and 2 rows long using 1 bead for the tops and bottoms and 2 beads for the sides.

Work the base of the necklace off this square, using the following column groups as your guide. Always add column separator units between columns and group separator columns between column groups:

Clasp column group 1: Weave 2 units for the first columns, 3 units for the second column, and 2 units for the third column.

Column groups 2–5: Weave 2 units for the first column, 3 units for the second column, and 2 units for the third column (figure 2). Repeat 3 more times for a total of 4 groups.

Column group 6: Weave 3 units for the first column, 5 units for the second column, and 3 units for the third column.

Column group 7: Weave 2 units, 3 units, and 2 units.

Column group 8: Weave 4 units, 6 units, and 4 units.

Column group 9: Weave 2 units, 3 units, and 2 units.

Column group 10: Weave 5 units, 7 units, and 5 units to create the necklace's center.

Column groups 11–18: Repeat column groups 1–9 in reverse to stitch the other side of the necklace, creating an 18-inch (45.7 cm)-long base. Don't trim the thread.

Continued on next page

SUPPLIES

Basic Beading Kit (page 10)

Crystal 6-pound braided beading thread

Matte metallic copper size 11° seed beads, 7 g

Matte metallic copper size 15° seed beads, 1.5 g

202 light Colorado topaz AB bicone crystal beads, 4 mm

51 copper AB fire-polished teardrop beads, 7 x 10 mm

1 transparent copper fire-polished rivoli with center-drilled vertical hole, 13 x 9 mm

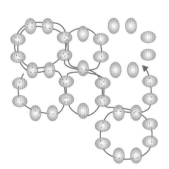

figure 1

figure 2

▶ 2. Embellishment

Start a new length of doubled thread that exits from the top edge beads of the third column from the right, from right to left. Pick up 1 size 15° bead, one 4-mm bicone crystal, and 1 size 15° bead. Pass through the 2 size 11° seed beads at the bottom of the same unit from right to left. Repeat on the next unit in the same column (figure 3).

Weave through the beadwork in order to repeat the bicone crystal embellishment on the next column. On the lower unit, pass through the first of the 2 beads on the bottom edge; pick up 1 size 11° bead, one 4-mm bicone crystal, 1 fire-polished teardrop, and 3 size 11° beads. Pass back

through the teardrop, the bicone crystal, the first size 11° bead just strung, and the next size 11° bead on the unit's bottom edge (figure 4).

Weave through the beads to repeat the bicone crystal embellishment on the next column.

Repeat until all 2-bead-wide columns are embellished.

▶ 3. Clasp

Orient the work horizontally so the embellished side faces up. Start a new single thread that exits down through the left side beads of the top unit in the first column of column group 1. Pick up 24 size 11° beads and pass through the left side beads of the bottom unit in the third column. Weave through several adjacent beads and pass back through the last size 11° added. Add 1 size 11° bead between every other bead on the original loop. Pass back through the original size 11° bead, weave in the thread, and trim (figure 5).

Start a new thread at the other end of the necklace, exiting from the mirror bead where the clasp loop was placed. Pick up the rivoli, 1 size 11° bead, and 3 size 15° beads. Pass back through the size 11° and the rivoli and weave through the base beads (figure 6). Repeat the thread path to reinforce. Weave in the thread and trim.

figure 3

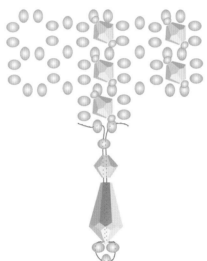

figure 4

figure 5

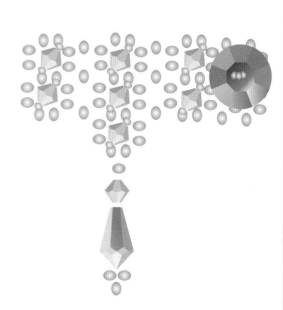

figure 6

SUPPLIES

Basic Beading Kit (page 10)

Antique copper size 11°
metal seed beads, 3 g

177 dark bronze fire-polished
glass beads, 3 mm

114 semiprecious turquoise
round beads, 3 mm

Bronze metallic size 15°
seed beads, 1 g

1 semiprecious turquoise
nugget, 16 x 21 mm

Copper .019-diameter
flexible beading wire,
32 inches (81.3 cm) long

10 Bali-style antiqued
copper metallic spacers,
5.5 x 5 mm

7 semiprecious turquoise
nuggets, 10–15 mm

4 copper crimp tubes,
2 x 2 mm

2 copper crimp covers, 3 mm

Wire cutters

Crimping tool

Chain-nose pliers

GABRIELLA

The striking geometry of this pendant makes it an instant attention-getter.

Its graceful arch and the turquoise stone dangling from the diamond drop

lend an ethnic flair for yet more drama.

▶ 1. Arch

Work a strip of right angle weave 5 units long, using 2 size 11° beads for the top, bottom, and sides of each unit. For units 7 through 13, use 3 size 11° beads for the top, 2 for the bottom, and 2 for the sides of each unit. Work units 14 through 19 units with 2 beads for the top, 2 beads for the bottom, and 2 beads for the sides of each unit.

Continued on next page

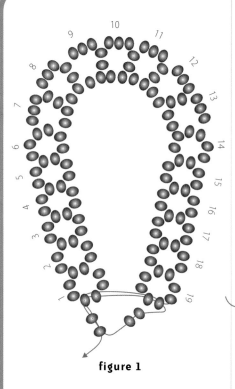

figure 1

Pass through the 2 bottom beads of unit 19 from right to left. Pass through the 2 bottom beads of unit 1 from right to left. Pick up 4 size 11° beads and pass through the 2 bottom beads of unit 19, the 2 bottom beads of unit 1, and the first 2 of the beads just added (figure 1).

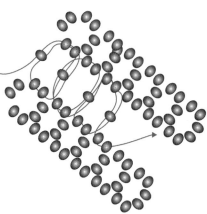

figure 3

▶ 2. Diamond

Pick up 6 size 11° beads and pass through the 2 beads just exited to create the first right angle weave unit of the diamond. Repeat to add 4 more units. Turn the corner by exiting the 2 interior beads (formerly bottom beads) of the fifth unit. Work 4 more units to create the diamond's second side. Turn the corner as before and work 4 more units to make the diamond's third side. For the fourth side, turn the corner and complete 3 additional units. Join the final unit to the third and fourth beads you added in the original arch, adding only side beads to create the new unit (figure 2). Don't cut the thread. Set aside.

Repeat steps 1 and 2 to make a second base.

▶ 3. Layers

Hold the two bases with their inside edges aligned. Weave the working thread of one of the bases through the beads to exit from 2 interior edge beads. Pick up 1 size 11° bead and pass through the opposing interior edge beads on the second base. Pick up 1 size 11° bead and pass back through the edge beads you originally exited. Continue working right angle weave until all the inside edges are joined (figure 3; also see figure 20 in Fundamentals, page 23).

Repeat the join on the exterior edge using fire-polished beads (figure 4), with the exception of the diamond's three exposed corners, where you'll use size 11° beads.

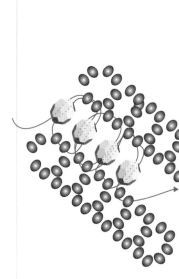

figure 2

figure 4

► 4. Embellishment

Weave through the beadwork to exit up through 2 side beads on the front of the base. Pick up 1 turquoise round bead and pass up through the 2 side beads of the next unit, creating a Z with the thread. This places the turquoise round bead diagonally across the empty space within the unit. Repeat until all the units on the front and back of the base have been embellished (figure 5).

Weave through the beadwork to exit from 2 beads on the edge of the front of the base. Pick up 1 size 15° bead and pass through the 2 edge beads of the next unit. Repeat around to embellish the interior and exterior edges of both the top and the bottom layers (figure 6; also see figure 21 in Fundamentals, page 24).

Weave the thread through the beads to exit from 2 size 11° beads on the top layer of the diamond's bottom point. Pick up 1 fire-polished bead, the 16 x 21 mm turquoise nugget, 1 fire-polished bead, and 3 size 15° beads. Pass back through the fire-polished bead, the turquoise nugget, and the fire-polished bead. Pull snug. Pass into the 2 size 11° beads on the bottom layer of the diamond's bottom point (figure 7).

Continued on next page

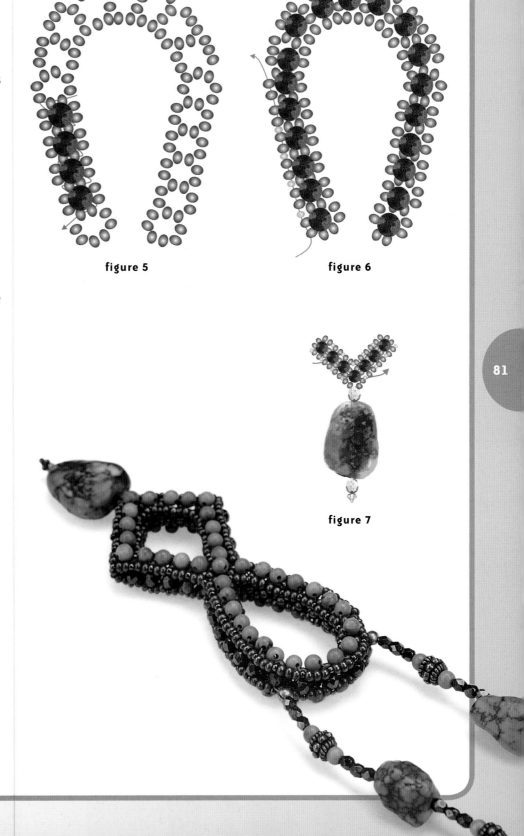

figure 5

figure 6

figure 7

81

▶ 5. Straps

Cut a 16-inch (40.6 cm) length of beading wire and slide on one crimp tube. Loop one wire end around the fire-polished bead that connects the top and bottom bases' eighth arch units. Leave a 1-inch (2.5 cm) tail. Pass back through the crimp tube and use crimping pliers to secure the tube. Use chain-nose pliers to gently squeeze a crimp cover over the tube.

String on a sequence of 3 fire-polished beads, 1 turquoise round bead, 1 spacer, 1 turquoise round bead, 3 fire-polished beads, and one 10–15 mm turquoise nugget 3 times (figure 8). String on 6 fire-polished beads. String on a sequence of 1 turquoise round bead, 1 spacer, 1 turquoise round bead, and 5 fire-polished beads 2 times. String on 3 turquoise round beads, 5 fire-polished beads, 1 turquoise round bead, 3 fire-polished beads, 1 turquoise round bead, 3 fire-polished beads, 1 turquoise round bead, 5 fire-polished beads, 1 turquoise round bead, 8 fire-polished beads, 1 turquoise round bead, 5 fire-polished beads, 1 turquoise round bead, 3 fire-polished beads, 1 turquoise round bead, 3 fire-polished beads, 1 crimp tube, one 10–15 mm turquoise nugget, 1 fire-polished bead, and 3 size 15° beads. Pass back through the fire-polished bead, nugget, and crimp tube. Snug the beads and crimp the tube.

Repeat the stringing sequence for the other side of the necklace, but instead of adding a nugget after the final crimp tube, string enough size 11° beads to pass over the nugget on the other strap. Pass back through the crimp tube and several of the fire-polished beads. Snug the beads and crimp the tube. Use chain-nose pliers to gently squeeze a crimp cover over the tube.

figure 8

82

URCHIN

With spines like a sea creature's, this beaded bead has a strikingly sculptural quality. You may be surprised to find that it's worked flat and then joined and embellished to create the ridged texture.

SUPPLIES FOR BEADED BEAD

Basic Beading Kit (page 10)

Smoke 6-pound braided beading thread

Metallic copper size 15° seed beads, 1 g

Aqua matte size 11° seed beads, 3.5 g

Dark brown size 8° seed beads, 4.5 g

42 turquoise 2XAB bicone crystal beads, 3 mm

SUPPLIES FOR NECKLACE

Basic Beading Kit (page 10)

Metallic copper AB size 11° seed beads, 3.5 g

Metallic copper size 15° seed beads, 6 g

36 turquoise 2XAB bicone crystal beads, 3 mm

1 antiqued copper hammered toggle ring, 22 mm

1 antiqued copper fancy toggle bar with hole, 30 mm

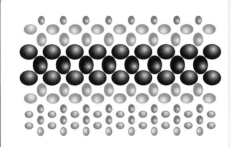

figure 1

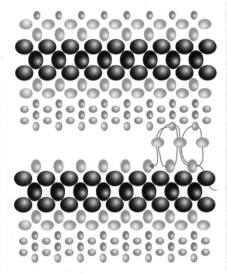

figure 2

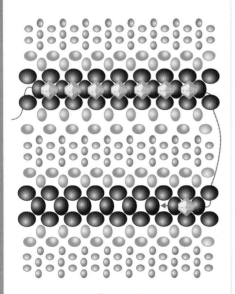

figure 3

figure 4

figure 5

figure 6

▶ 1. Base

Use doubled thread to work a strip of right angle weave 8 units wide by 35 rows long using the following bead types for each row:

Rows 1 and 2: Use size 15° beads.

Row 3: Use size 11° beads.

Row 4: Use size 8° beads.

Row 5: Use size 8° beads for the sides and size 11° beads for the tops of each unit.

Row 6: Use size 11° beads for the sides and size 15° beads for the top of each unit (figure 1).

Rows 7–30: Repeat rows 1–6 to create a total of 5 "spines."

Rows 31–35: Add a sixth spine by repeating rows 1–5 only.

Use size 11° beads to join the last row to the first row (figure 2; also see figure 20 in Fundamentals, page 23).

Note: If you have trouble passing through the size 15° beads, use a size 13 needle.

Also, when changing bead sizes it's easy to miss a bead in the previous row. I recommend carefully counting the beads you've added at the end of each row, making sure they total 8 units.

▶ 3. Spiral Cord

Use doubled thread to pick up 4 size 11° "core" beads and 4 size 15° "spiral" beads, leaving an 8-inch (20.3 cm) tail. Pass through the core beads again and push the spiral beads to the side (figure 4).

Pick up 1 core bead and 4 spiral beads. Pass through the last 3 core beads and the new core bead. Push the spiral beads to the side (figure 5).

Repeat this step to achieve the desired length, except on every twelfth repeat use one 3-mm crystal as your core bead and 5 size 15° beads as your spiral beads. Pass through the previous 3 core beads and the crystal. Push the spiral beads to the side (figure 6).

On one end of the spiral cord, pick up 5 size 15° beads and the toggle ring's loop. Pick up 5 more size 15° beads and pass back through the cord's core beads. Repeat the thread path to reinforce. Weave in the thread and trim. On the other end of the cord, use the tail thread to pick up 5 size 15° seed beads. Pass through the hole in the toggle bar and pick up one 3-mm crystal and 1 size 15° bead. Pass back through the crystal and the toggle bar. Pick up 5 size 15° beads and pass back through the cord's core beads (figure 7). Repeat the thread path to reinforce. Weave in the thread and trim.

Pass the toggle bar through your beaded bead.

figure 7

▶ 2. Embellishment

Orient the tube so the spines are vertical. Weave through the beadwork to exit from the first vertical-hole size 8° bead at the top of one of the spines. Pick up one 3-mm crystal bead and pass through the next vertical-hole size 8° bead. Pull tight so the crystal bead snaps into place between the 2 size 8° beads. Continue to add a total of 7 crystals to the spine. Without adding any beads, pass through the adjacent horizontal-hole size 8° bead in this spine and the horizontal-hole size 8° bead in the next spine. Pass through the vertical-hole size 8° bead in the new spine and add crystals between the size 8° beads as before (figure 3). Repeat until all spines have been embellished.

Pass through each horizontal-hole size 8° edge bead and pull tightly. Weave through the beadwork and repeat on the other side. Weave in the thread and trim. Set the beaded bead aside.

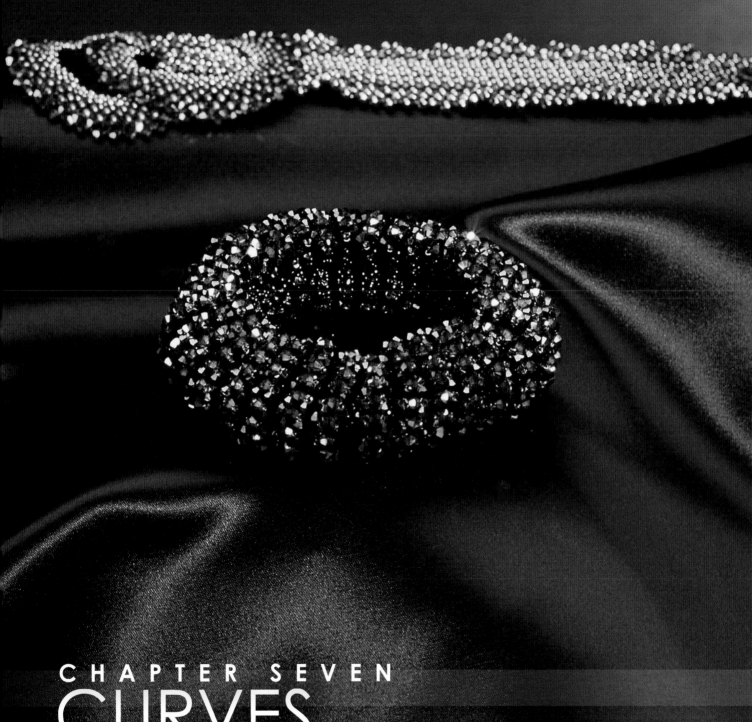

CHAPTER SEVEN

CURVES

FANFARE

A profusion of crystals makes this bracelet a real sparkler, catching so much light that it becomes the life of the party. Its design looks deceivingly complex at first glance—but it simply consists of many of the same components strung together on gossamer floss to create a seamless cuff.

▶ 1. Fans

Row 1: Use doubled thread and size 15° beads to weave a strip of right angle weave 25 units long. **Note:** If you have trouble weaving through the size 15° beads, use a size 13 needle.

Row 2: Work right angle weave using size 11° beads.

Row 3: Work right angle weave using A beads (figure 1).

Join the beadwork into a circle by adding the top and bottom beads, matching the bead size to the row you're joining (figure 2; also see figure 20 in Fundamentals, page 23).

Continued on next page

figure 1

figure 2

SUPPLIES

Basic Beading Kit (page 10)

Smoke 6-pound braided beading thread

Shiny black size 15° seed beads, 11 g

Shiny black size 11° seed beads, 21 g

1664 black bicone crystal beads, 3 mm (A)

384 jet AB2X bicone crystal beads, 3 mm (B)

Gossamer elastic floss, 48 inches (1.2 m)

Clear watchmaker's cement

Big-eyed needle

Fold the strip in half lengthwise. Note the B beads marked with arrows in figure 3; they will be opposite one another.

Weave through the beadwork to exit from the top A bead, second from the end. Use B beads to join the 2 top A beads (figure 4; also see figure 20 in Fundamentals, page 23). Weave in the thread and trim.

Repeat this step to equal your wrist measurement plus 1 inch (2.5 cm). **Note:** Four fans equal approximately 1 inch (2.5 cm) of bracelet length. (The bracelet shown is made with 32 fans equaling 8 inches [20.3 cm], but fits a 7-inch [17.8 cm] wrist perfectly.)

▶ 2. Assembly

Thread the big-eyed needle with 12 inches (30.5 cm) of doubled gossamer floss. String the fans to one another by passing through the opening created between the second units of rows 2 and 3 (see the bottom arrow in figure 5 for placement). Tie a strong knot, trim, and add a dab of watchmaker's cement. When dry, slide the knot inside an adjacent fan. Repeat to connect the other end of the fans, passing through the point marked by the top arrow in figure 5.

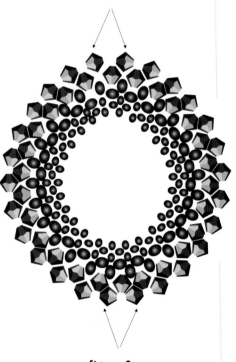

figure 3

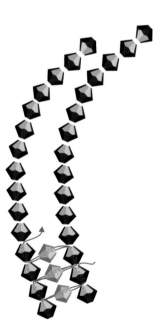

figure 4

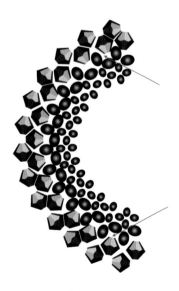

figure 5

SUPPLIES

Basic Beading Kit (page 10)

Smoke 6-pound braided beading thread

Metallic bronze size 15° seed beads, 1 g

Size 11° seed beads:
Matte metallic blue, 1.5 g (A)
Metallic bronze, 3 g (D)

Size 8° seed beads:
Matte metallic blue, 5 g (B)
Metallic bronze, 8 g (C)

152 Dorado bicone crystal beads, 3 mm

2 black sewing snaps, ¹/₄ inch (6 mm)

ENTWINED CIRCLES

Overlapping circles rest gracefully on the wrist, serving as the base for a hidden closure to create a seamless bracelet. Different size beads create the gentle curves.

▶ 1. Circles

Row 1: Use doubled thread and size 15° beads to weave a strip of right angle weave 37 units long. If you have trouble passing through the size 15° beads you can use a size 13 needle.

Row 2: Use A beads to work right angle weave across the row.

Row 3: Use B beads to work right angle weave across the row.

Row 4: Use bicone crystals to work right angle weave across the row (figure 1).

Continued on next page

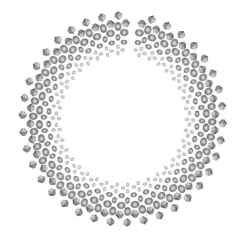

figure 1

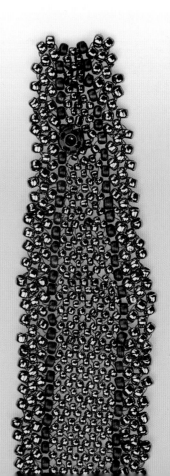

Join the strip into a circle by adding the top and bottom beads, matching the bead type to the row you're joining (figure 2; also see figure 20 in Fundamentals, page 23).

Complete a second circle using the same beads and counts, but before closing the join, insert it into the center of the first circle (figure 3). Complete the join (figure 4). Set the circles aside.

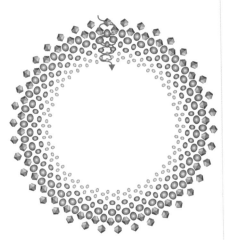

figure 2

figure 3

▶ **2. Base**

Start a strip of right angle weave 5 units wide with the following bead types in each unit

Unit 1: Use C beads.

Unit 2: Use B beads for the top and bottom and 1 D bead for the side.

Unit 3: Use D beads.

Unit 4: Use B beads for the top and bottom and C for the side.

Unit 5: Use C beads.

Continue in this pattern, increasing by 1 D-bead unit in the middle of every fourth row until you have increased 4 times for a total of 5 center D-bead units and 9 total units (figure 5; also see figure 22 in Fundamentals, page 24). Weave in the thread and trim. Set the strip aside.

Repeat to create a second identical strip, but continue working rows until the combined measurement of the strips equals ½ inch (1.3 cm) less than your wrist measurement. Join the 9-unit ends of the 2 strips together to make 1 long strip (see figure 20 in Fundamentals, page 23). Weave in the thread and trim.

▶ 3. Closures

Position one end of the strip over the left circle and weave it under the right circle so its edge meets the interior edge of the right circle. Sew the strip's edge to the interior and exterior edges of the right circle. Weave in the thread and trim. Start a new thread where the strip intersects the left circle; stitch the strip to the circle's interior and exterior edges. Weave in the thread and trim.

Keep the strip untwisted as you position the other end over the right circle and under the left circle so the strip's end meets the left circle's interior edge. Mark the strip/circle meeting points; sew one half of a snap to the back of the left circle and the other half to the top of the strip's end. Sew the remaining snap so it connects the front of the right circle to the back of the strip (figure 6). **Note:** The snaps shown in figure 6 are for placement reference only. The snaps will lie between the strip and the circles and won't show.

figure 4

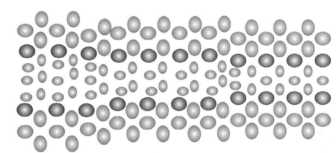

figure 5

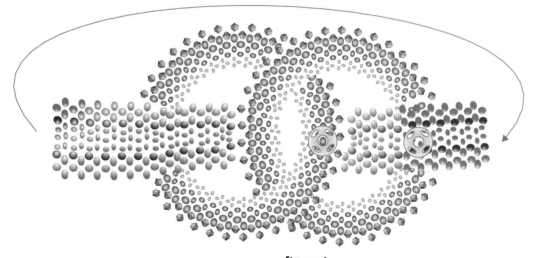

figure 6

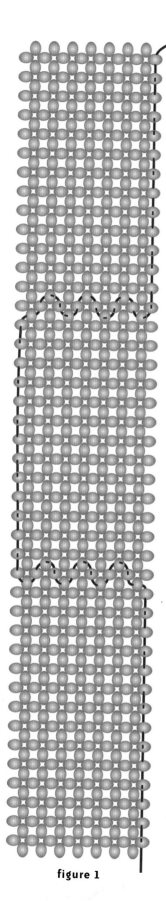

figure 1

SHADOW WAVE

Sinuous ripples of bead fabric play off the colors

of a pendant embellished with a crystal rivoli.

▶ **1. Strap**

Use A beads to create a strip of right angle weave 7 units wide and 114 rows long. Switch to B beads, with an occasional A bead mixed in, and continue for an additional 114 rows to make a 21½-inch (54.6 cm) finished necklace.

Weave through 14 beads along one long edge of the strap, adding no beads between. Pull the thread gently to introduce a graceful curve in the beadwork. Weave through the beads at the strap's center and exit from the fifteenth edge bead at the other side of the strap. Pass through 14 edge beads, pull the thread gently to form a curve, and weave through the beadwork to the other side of the strap. Continue gathering the piece into curves until all edge beads have been used (figure 1).

Continued on next page

SUPPLIES

Basic Beading Kit (page 10)

Size 11° seed beads:
    Metallic gold iris, 17 g (A)
    Cranberry, 17 g (B)

Mix of metallic gold and copper size 15° seed beads, 1 g (C)

1 volcano triangular crystal rivoli, 23 mm

16 dark maroon freshwater pearl beads, 3 mm

2 black sewing snaps, ¼ inch (6 mm)

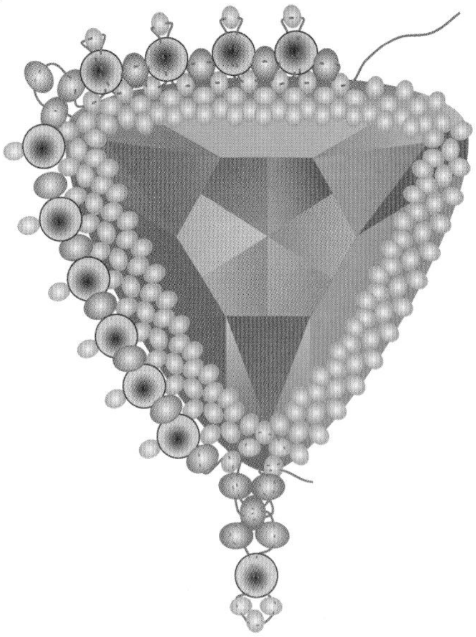

figure 2

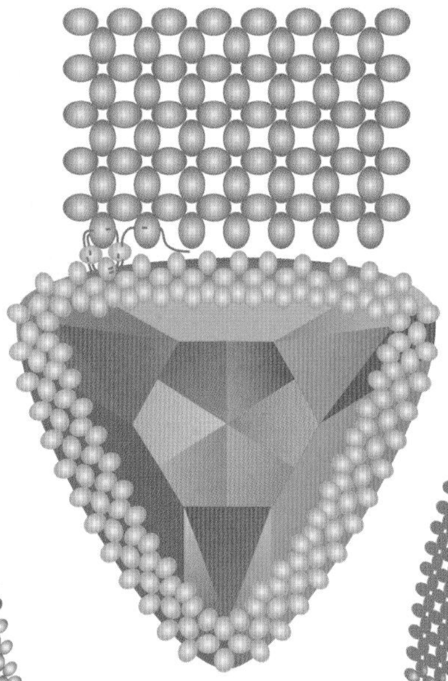

figure 3

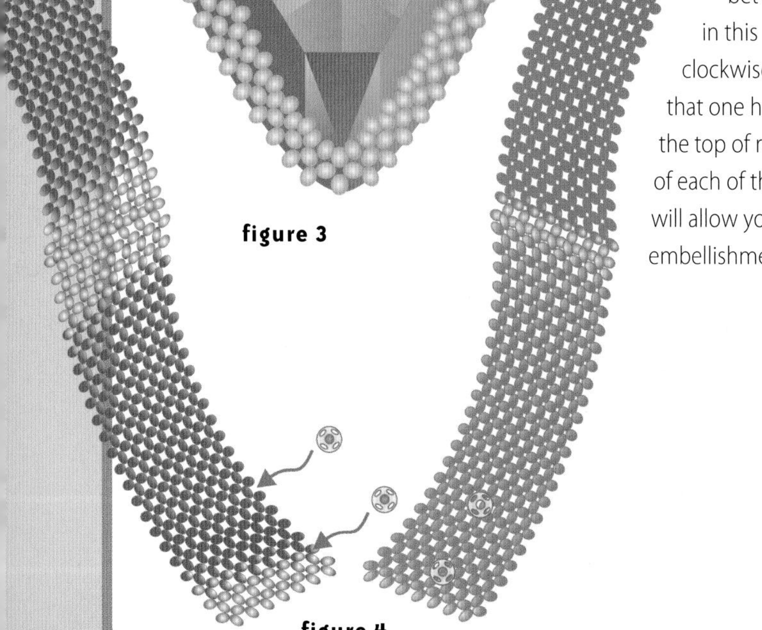

figure 4

▶ 2. Bezel

Use C beads to make a strip of right angle weave wide enough to fit around the edge of your rivoli. Use an odd number of units so that when joined you will have an even number of spaces. Test the size. The strip should fit around the edge of the rivoli with only a slight space between each end. Make your strip 4 rows long. Join the short ends together (see figure 20 in Fundamentals, page 23).

Exiting from an edge bead, weave through the last round's edge beads without adding beads between. This will pull the ring into a cup-shaped bezel. Hold the cup with the round you just pulled tight on the bottom and place the rivoli into the cup, right side up.

Weave through the beads to exit from an edge bead on the other side of the bezel. Pass through each edge bead as you did for the back of the bezel. If the bezel is too tight, you may need to add 1 C bead between each 1 or 2 beads in this round. Slide the bezel clockwise around the rivoli so that one horizontal-hole bead at the top of round 1 is on both sides of each of the rivoli's corners. This will allow you to make the corner embellishments.

▶ 3. Bezel Embellishment

Weave through beads to exit from a horizontal-hole bead in round 2 at one of the corners. Pick up 3 B beads and pass through the next horizontal-hole bead on the bezel. Weave through the beads to exit from the second B just added. Pick up 1 B bead, 1 pearl bead, and 3 C beads. Pass back through the pearl. Pick up 1 B bead and pass through the second and third B beads originally added in this step and the next horizontal-hole bead on the bezel.

Pick up 1 pearl bead and 1 C bead. Pass back through the pearl bead and pass through the next horizontal-hole bead on the bezel. Pick up 1 B bead and pass through the next horizontal-hole bead on the bezel. Continue across to the bezel's second corner, where you will embellish with 3 B beads only (figure 2). Repeat for the third side.

▶ 4. Join

Join the top of the triangular bezel to the last row at one end of the necklace, making sure the longer fringe embellishment is at the bottom corner (figure 3; also see figure 20 in Fundamentals, page 23).

▶ 5. Closure

Overlap the two strap ends. Securely stitch the snaps between the layers, 1 inch (2.5 cm) apart (figure 4).

SUPPLIES

Basic Beading Kit (page 10)

Smoke 6-pound braided beading thread

Purple size 11° seed beads, 8 g

72 amethyst AB round crystal beads, 4 mm

Bronze size 15° seed beads, 1.5 g

72 jet AB2X bicone crystal beads, 4 mm

24 Dorado bicone crystal beads, 3 mm

24 blue iris fire-polished beads, 3 mm

24 purple freshwater pearls, 3 mm

1 black sewing snap, ¼ inch (6 mm)

97

TERRACITA

The circular medallions in this piece are reminiscent of vintage costume jewelry.

You can alter the embellishments to create any number of different looks.

Sizing

This bracelet can be sized as follows:

Small: 5 medallions (6¾ inches [17.1 cm])

Medium: 5 medallions made with the full 2 rounds and 1 medallion made with round 1 only (7½ inches [19.1 cm])

Large: 6 medallions (8 inches [20.3 cm])

figure 1

figure 2

figure 3

figure 7

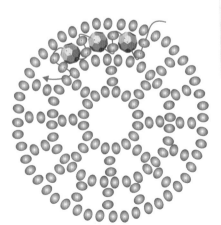

figure 4

▶ 1. Medallions

Base: Use single thread to pick up 16 size 11° beads. Tie an overhand knot to form a circle (figure 1). Pass through 2 beads to the right of the knot.

Round 1: Pick up 8 size 11° beads and pass through the last 2 base beads you exited, making a counterclockwise circle. Pass through the first 2 beads just added (these are your side beads). Pick up 6 size 11° beads, make a clockwise circle, and pass back through the next 2 beads on the base, 2 shared side beads of the first unit, and the 4 top and 2 side beads added in this unit (figure 2). Continue to add 5 more units. Join the seventh and first units with 4 top beads, creating an eighth unit.

Round 2: Use size 11° beads to work 16 units of right angle weave off of round 1; each unit should consist of 2 bottom beads, 2 side beads, and 3 top beads (figure 3). Join the first and last units with 3 top beads. Weave in your thread and trim.

▶ 2. Medallion Embellishment

Start a doubled thread that exits from 2 side beads in round 2, toward the center. Pick up a 4-mm round crystal and pass through the next 2 side beads from top to bottom, toward the center of the medallion. Repeat until you've added a total of 16 crystals (figure 4).

Weave through the beadwork to exit from 2 top beads in round 1. Pick up 3 size 15° beads and pass through the next 2 round 1 size 11° beads to form a picot. Repeat to add a total of 16 picots (figure 5).

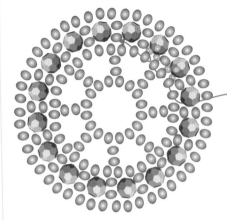

figure 5

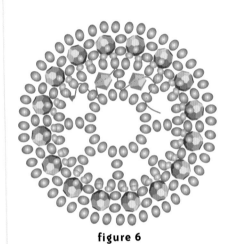

figure 6

Pass through beads to exit from 2 side beads in round 1, toward the medallion's edge. Pick up a 4-mm bicone crystal and pass through the next set of side beads from bottom to top. Repeat to add 8 crystals in all (figure 6).

Weave through the beads to exit from 2 seed beads in the base. Pass through the next 2 base beads (figure 7). Pick up a 3-mm bicone crystal, skip 2 base beads, and pass through the next 2 base beads. Continue until you have added 4 crystals.

Pick up a 3-mm fire-polished bead and pass through the next 3-mm bicone crystal added to the base. Repeat to add a total of 4 fire-polished beads (figure 8). Pass through all the bicone crystals and fire-polished beads to reinforce.

▶ 3. Shaping

Weave through the beadwork to the outside edge of round 2. Pass through all the size 11° beads on the outside edge and pull tightly to cup the medallion. Weave the thread into the base of the medallion (not the edge beads) and trim.

Repeat steps 1 through 3 for the total number of medallions required for your size (see Sizing, page 97). Repeat the embellishment pattern twice for a total of 3 medallions; for the others, reverse the 2 embellishment rounds that use 4-mm round crystals and 4-mm bicone crystals.

▶ 4. Join

Lay the medallions in the proper order on your work surface. Start a new thread on the first medallion that exits from 2 edge beads adjacent to 2 side beads. (You may find this easier to see from the underside of the medallion.) Pick up 6 size 11° beads and make a clockwise circle to pass through the 2 beads you just exited and the first 2 beads just strung. Pick up 4 size 11° beads, make a counterclockwise circle to pass through the next 2 edge beads of the medallion, the 2 side beads of the first unit, and the 2 top beads of the unit just added. Pick up 2 size 11°

beads and pass through 2 edge beads on a second medallion, making sure they're adjacent to a set of side beads. Pick up 2 size 11° beads and pass through the 2 beads on the top of the second unit, the 2 side beads of unit 3, the 2 edge beads of the second medallion, the 2 side beads just added, and the 2 top beads of the first unit. Pick up 2 size 11° beads and pass through the next 2 edge beads on the second medallion (figure 9).

Continued on next page

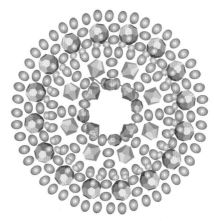

figure 8

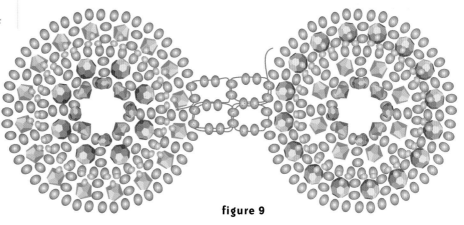

figure 9

figure 10

figure 11

▶ 5. Join Embellishment

Use 3-mm pearls to embellish the join diagonally across the units just added. Weave through the beadwork to exit up from the center of the 4 units. Pick up a 4-mm bicone crystal and 1 size 15° bead. Pass back through the 4-mm bicone crystal and weave through the beadwork to form a fringe.

Weave through the beads to the other side of the second medallion and join it to a third medallion. Repeat to connect all the medallions (figure 10).

▶ 6. Clasp

On the other side of the first medallion, stitch 4 units of right angle weave the same as you did in step 4, but add 2 top beads to complete the third and fourth units. Embellish as you did in step 5, and securely sew half of the snap to the underside of the units. Weave in the thread and trim.

At the other end of the bracelet, exit from 2 top beads that lie opposite the join between the last 2 medallions. Pick up 1 size 11° bead, skip an edge bead, and pass through the next edge bead. Pick up 1 size 11° bead, skip an edge bead, and pass through the following one. Pick up 1 size 11° bead and pass back through the previous size 11° bead placed. Pick up 1 size 11° bead and pass back through the first size 11° bead placed. Continue working peyote stitch in this manner for a total of 6 rows. Securely sew the remaining snap half to the top of the peyote-stitched tab (figure 11). Weave in the thread and trim.

SUPPLIES

Basic Beading Kit (page 10)

Smoke 6-pound braided beading thread

Black size 15° seed beads, 1.5 g (A)

Size 11° seed beads:
    Black, 1.5 g (B)
    Matte black, < 0.5 g (C)

104 black bicone crystals, 3 mm

2 black baroque teardrop crystals, 11 x 16 mm

Chain-nose pliers

Sterling silver ear wires, 2

WHITBY

Although these elegant earrings feature an elaborate beaded oval, the project doesn't at all require advanced beadwork skills. The oval's gentle curves are produced by simply increasing the bead size in each row.

▶ 1. Circle

Row 1: Use doubled thread and A beads to weave a strip of right angle weave 25 units long and 1 row high. If you have trouble going through the size 15° beads, use a size 13 needle.

Row 2: Use B beads to work right angle weave across the row.

Row 3: Use bicone crystals to work right angle weave across the row (figure 1).

Join the strip into a flat circle by adding 1 bicone crystal in the top position and 1 B bead in the bottom position, connecting the beginning and end units of this row (see figure 20, Fundamentals, page 23). Weave through the beadwork to exit from a side bead at the end of row 2. Pass through the side bead at the beginning of row 2. This will help create a point at the top of the earring, rather than a circle, since you aren't adding the top and bottom beads as usual. Repeat to connect the beginning and end side beads of row 1 (figure 2).

▶ 2. Loop

Weave through adjacent beads to exit up through the vertical bicone crystal to one side of the join. Pick up 7 A beads and pass back through the bicone crystal.

▶ 3. Dangle

Weave through the beadwork to exit through the vertical bicone crystal directly opposite the ear wire loop just added. Pick up 3 A beads, 1 teardrop, and 3 A beads. Pass back through the vertical bicone crystal last exited (figure 3). Use chain-nose pliers to attach an ear wire to the loop.

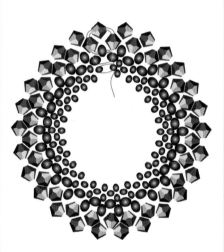

figure 2

figure 3

ROW

3

2

1

figure 1

▶ 4. Embellishment

Weave through the beads to exit from a horizontal B bead in row 2. String 1 C bead and pass through the next horizontal B bead in row 2. Repeat around to add a total of 25 C beads. Turn the earring over and repeat the embellishment on the other side (figure 4; also see figure 21, Fundamentals, page 24).

figure 4

The Whitby earrings are each composed of a pair of curves. If you take that technique further, you can achieve something as dramatic as this *Victoria* necklace.

CHAPTER EIGHT

LAYERS

AMPHORA

To create the bold shape of this bead, make a tubular base of right angle weave, changing bead sizes as you work each round.

▶ 1. Base

Right angle weave a tube following figure 1 for bead types placement. ***Note:*** To make the bead symmetrical, rows 8 and 10 have different side and top beads (figure 1).

Base round 1: Use A beads to work a strip of right angle weave 11 units long. Join the first and last units to create 12-unit ring (see figures 17 and 18 in Fundamentals, page 22).

Base round 2: Use all A beads to work tubular right angle weave.

Base rounds 3 and 4: Repeat row 2 using G beads.

Base rounds 5–7: Repeat row 2 using C beads.

Base round 8: Repeat row 2 using C beads for the sides and G beads for the tops.

Base round 9: Repeat row 2 using G beads.

Base round 10: Repeat row 2 using G beads for the sides and A beads for the tops.

Base rounds 11 and 12: Repeat row 2 using A beads. Exit from a horizontal A bead.

Continued on next page

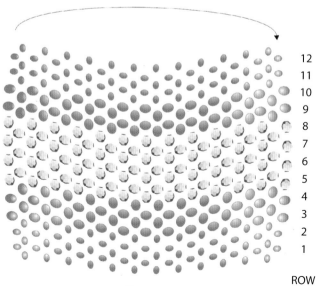

12
11
10
9
8
7
6
5
4
3
2
1

ROW

figure 1

SUPPLIES

Basic Beading Kit (page 10)

Smoke 6-pound braided beading thread

Size 11° seed beads:
    Bronze, 1.5 g (A)
    Silver-lined aqua, < 0.5 g (B)

86 bronze fire-polished beads, 3 mm (C)

24 olivine AB2X bicone crystal beads, 3 mm (D)

24 turquoise AB2X bicone crystal beads, 3mm (E)

Bronze size 15° seed beads, 0.5 g (F)

Size 8° seed beads:
    Bronze, 6 g (G)
    Matte pink/gold, < 0.5 g (H)

6.2-mm-diameter metal mesh chain necklace, 28 inches (71.1 cm) long

▶ 2. Layer Two: Horizontal Beads

Embellish the base with beads to set up for right angle weave in the next step. Follow figure 2 for bead placement (also see figure 21 in Fundamentals, page 24).

Layer 2, round 1: String 1 A bead and pass through the next horizontal bead of base round 12. Repeat to add a total of 12 A beads. Weave through the beadwork to exit from a horizontal base round 2 bead.

Layer 2, rounds 2 and 3: Repeat round 2 using B beads.

Layer 2, rounds 4–10: Repeat round 2 using G beads.

Layer 2, rounds 11 and 12: Repeat round 2 using B beads.

Layer 2, round 13: Repeat round 2 using A beads.

▶ 3. Layer Two: Vertical Beads

Weave through beads to exit from a layer 2, round 12 bead. With the beaded bead oriented with the hole horizontal, join the tops of the layer 2 rounds as follows (figure 3; also see figure 20 in Fundamentals, page 23):

Use A beads to join layer 2, rounds 12 and 11. Pass through the adjacent G bead between base rounds 11 and 10 and into a layer 2, round 10 bead to step up to the next round.

In the same manner, use E beads to join layer 2 rounds 10 and 9. Exit from a layer 2, round 9 bead.

Use 1 F, 1 D, and 1 F bead on each side to join layer 2, rounds 9 and 8. Exit from a layer 2, round 8 bead.

Use 1 F, 1 H, and 1 F bead on each side to join layer 2, rounds 8 and 7.

To join layer 2, rounds 7 and 6, repeat the join for layer 2, rounds 8 and 7; for layer 2, rounds 6 and 5, repeat the join for layer 2, rounds 9 and 8; for layer 2, rounds 5 and 4, repeat the join for layer 2, rounds

10 and 9. Weave through the adjacent G bead between base rounds 4 and 3. Exit from a layer 2, round 3 bead. Repeat the join for layer 2, rounds 12 and 11, connecting rounds 2 and 3. Weave in the thread and trim.

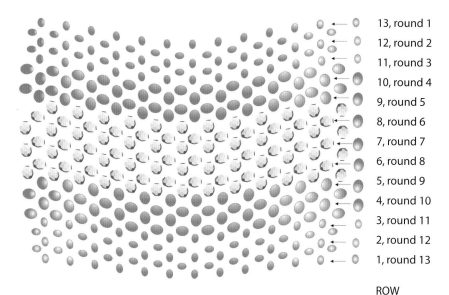

13, round 1
12, round 2
11, round 3
10, round 4
9, round 5
8, round 6
7, round 7
6, round 8
5, round 9
4, round 10
3, round 11
2, round 12
1, round 13

ROW

figure 2

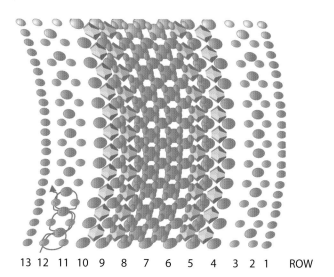

13 12 11 10 9 8 7 6 5 4 3 2 1 ROW

figure 3

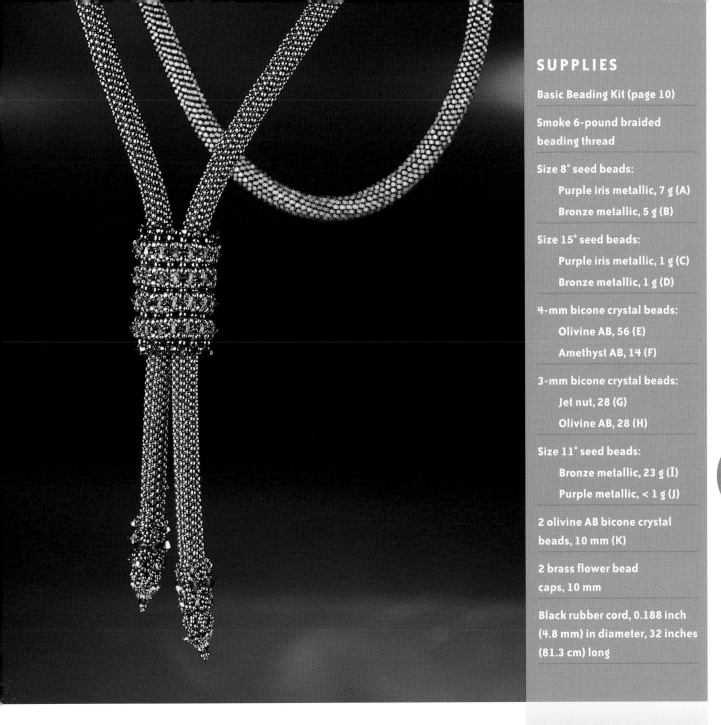

SUPPLIES

Basic Beading Kit (page 10)

Smoke 6-pound braided beading thread

Size 8° seed beads:
 Purple iris metallic, 7 g (A)
 Bronze metallic, 5 g (B)

Size 15° seed beads:
 Purple iris metallic, 1 g (C)
 Bronze metallic, 1 g (D)

4-mm bicone crystal beads:
 Olivine AB, 56 (E)
 Amethyst AB, 14 (F)

3-mm bicone crystal beads:
 Jet nut, 28 (G)
 Olivine AB, 28 (H)

Size 11° seed beads:
 Bronze metallic, 23 g (I)
 Purple metallic, < 1 g (J)

2 olivine AB bicone crystal beads, 10 mm (K)

2 brass flower bead caps, 10 mm

Black rubber cord, 0.188 inch (4.8 mm) in diameter, 32 inches (81.3 cm) long

DECO

Reminiscent of a bolo tie, this necklace features a crystal-studded slide that slips

onto a cord covered in right angle weave, its ends tapering into matched points.

▶ 1. Base Tube

Use A beads to create a strip of right angle weave 13 units wide and 9 rows long. Join into a tube (see figure 19 in Fundamentals, page 22).

▶ 2. Layer Two: Horizontal Beads

Embellish the edge rounds using G beads and the middle 8 rounds with B beads (figure 1; also see figure 21 in Fundamentals, page 24). Weave in the thread and trim.

▶ 3. Layer Two: Vertical Beads

Start a new doubled thread that exits from a B bead in round 1, from left to right. Pick up 1 C, 1 E, and 1 C bead. Working counterclockwise, pass through the adjacent B bead from round 2, below the one you last exited. Pick up 1 C, 1 E, and 1 C bead

and pass through the B bead originally exited in this step to complete 1 right angle weave unit. Weave through the beads to exit up through the second E bead added.

Pick up 1 C bead and pass through the next B bead in round 1. Pick up 1 C, 1 E, and 1 C bead. Pass through the adjacent B bead from round 2. Pick up 1 C bead and pass up through the side E and C beads from the previous unit, the top B bead of the next unit, and the following C and E beads to complete the second unit.

Repeat to connect base rounds 1 and 2. When the round is complete, weave through beads to exit a B bead in round 3. In the same manner, connect rounds 3 and 4, rounds 5 and 6, and rounds 7 and 8 for a total of 4 rounds of crystal joins (figure 2; also see figure 20 in Fundamentals, page 23). Weave in the thread and trim. Set aside.

▶ 4. Rope

Use doubled thread and I beads to work a strip of right angle weave 6 units wide and 32 inches (81.3 cm) long. Join the units over the rubber cord to make a filled beaded rope (see figure 20 in Fundamentals, page 23). Slide the ends of the rope through the slide completed in step 3.

▶ 5. Rope Ends

Use J beads to embellish the first 7 rounds of the rope (see figure 21 in Fundamentals, page 24).

Weave through the beadwork to exit a J bead in the seventh round. Join the J beads as you did with the slide in step 3, using 1 C bead, one 4-mm bicone crystal, and 1 C bead for each side, but this time use H beads for the crystals in the first set of joins, F beads for the middle set, and H beads for the last set (figure 3).

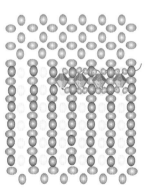

figure 3

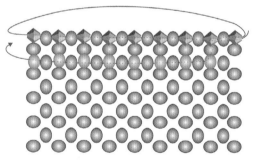

figure 1

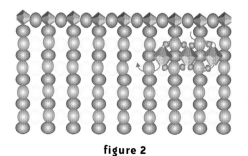

figure 2

Weave through the beads to exit from a J bead in round 1. Pick up 7 D beads and pass through the next J bead in the round. Repeat 5 more times for a total of 6 picots (figure 4). Pass through the first 4 beads added in the first picot.

Pick up 3 D beads and pass through the middle bead of the next picot added in figure 4. Pick up 1 J bead and pass through the middle bead of the next picot. Repeat around the tube, alternating between 3 D beads and 1 J bead (figure 5). Pass through the first 2 beads added in this step. Insert a K bead inside the net and pull the thread tight.

Pick up 3 D beads and pass through the middle bead of the next picot. Repeat 2 more times. Pass through the first 2 beads added in this step. Pass through the middle bead of the next 2 picots and pull tight. Pick up 1 bead cap, 1 F bead, and 3 D beads. Pass back through the F bead, the bead cap, and the D bead opposite the one you originally exited (figure 6). Repeat the thread path to secure. Weave in the thread and trim.

Repeat this step to embellish the other cord end.

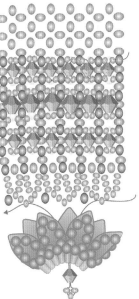

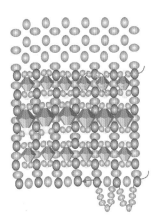

figure 4

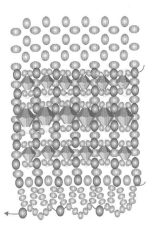

figure 5

figure 6

QUETZAL

The glamour of a cocktail ring is displayed in this architectural bit of eye candy. Light reflects from tiny Swarovski crystals to highlight the ring's edge and its layered dome.

SUPPLIES

Basic Beading Kit (page 10)

Size 11° seed beads:
   Matte gold, 1 g (A)
   Bronze, 3 g (B)

58 fuchsia round crystal beads, 2 mm

Size 15° seed beads:
   Fuchsia-lined clear,
   < 0.5 g (C)

Bronze, 8 (D)

Note: To layer the embellishment beads in this project, it's particularly helpful to reference both the text and the illustrations.

▶ 1. Ring Top Base

Use A beads to work a square of right angle weave 7 units wide and 7 rows long. Weave through the beads to exit through the bottom bead of the last unit added in row 7 from right to left.

▶ 2. Layer Two: Horizontal Beads

Embellish the base with beads to set up for right angle weave in the next step. Pick up 1 B bead and pass through the bottom bead of the next unit. Repeat until you have added a total of 6 beads. Pass through the side bead of the last unit from row 6 and the bottom bead of that same unit, from left to right. Continue to add 6 B beads across each of the rows (figure 1; also see figure 21 in Fundamentals, page 24). Weave through the beads to exit from the last bead placed, from left to right.

▶ 3. Layer Two: Vertical Beads

Use A beads to work off the horizontal B beads placed in step 2 to complete the second layer of right angle weave units. Pick up 1 A bead and pass through the horizontal B bead directly above the one you just exited. Pick up 1 A bead and pass through the B bead you originally exited. Pass through the first A bead just placed, the top horizontal B bead, the second A bead just placed, and the next horizontal B bead in the row to complete the first unit. Continue across the rows, adding vertical side beads to the horizontal beads for a total of 5 rows of joining. At the end of each row pass through a side bead in the base and the first horizontal bead in the next row (figure 2; also see figure 20 in Fundamentals, page 23).

Continued on next page

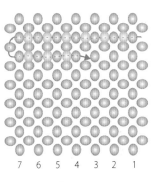

7 6 5 4 3 2 1   ROW

figure 1

figure 2

113

▶ 4. Layer Three: Vertical Beads

Pass through the top horizontal B bead and the right side A bead of the last unit. Pick up 1 B bead and pass through the next side A bead in the previous row. Repeat to add a total of 4 B beads. At the end of the column, pass through the horizontal B bead from the previous layer and the adjacent A side bead in the next column. Continue adding B beads to add a total of 5 rows (figure 3). At the end of the last row, pass through the horizontal B bead from the previous layer, the adjacent A side bead, and the B bead just added.

▶ 5. Layer Three: Horizontal Beads

In this layer the rows of vertical B beads placed in the last step will serve as the side bead for the join. Use A beads to join the rows as in step 3, repeating for a total of 4 rows (figure 4).

▶ 6. Layer Four: Horizontal Beads

Pass through the top bead of the last unit you joined. Pick up 1 B bead and pass through the next A bead. Repeat for a total of 3 B beads across the row. At the end of the row, pass through the vertical B bead in the previous layer and the horizontal A bead in the next row. Repeat to add horizontal B beads for a total of 3 rows (figure 5).

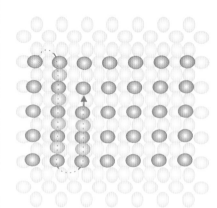

figure 3

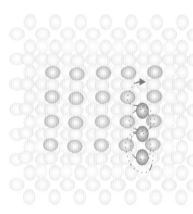

figure 4

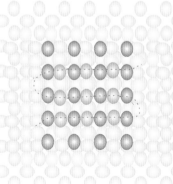

figure 5

▶ 7. Layer Four: Vertical Beads

Use 2-mm crystal beads as the side beads to join the horizontal B beads of the previous step for a total of 2 rows of joining.

Weave through the beads to exit from a layer 4 edge bead. Pick up one 2-mm crystal bead and pass through the next layer 4 edge bead. Repeat to embellish layer 4 on all 4 sides (figure 6). Weave in the thread and trim. Set the ring top aside.

▶ 8. Ring Mount

Use A beads to work a square of right angle weave 7 units wide and 7 rows long. Position this piece below the ring top and use 2-mm crystal beads and right angle weave to join the two pieces on all 4 edges (figure 7; also see figure 20 in Fundamentals, page 23). Weave through the beads to exit from the mount layer's third edge bead from the corner.

▶ 9. Ring Band

Pick up 3 B beads and pass through the edge bead last exited. Use B beads to work right angle weave, incorporating 2 more of the edge beads, to start a ring band that's centered in the middle of the mount. Continue to work rows of right angle weave off this base until the band is long enough to fit your finger. Join the band to the middle 3 edge beads on the opposite side of the mount (figure 8).

To embellish the band, exit a bottom bead of the final row. Pick up 1 D bead and pass through the next bottom bead. Repeat once. Weave to exit the bottom bead of the third-to-last band row and repeat, adding 2 D beads (figure 9).

Exit from one of the D beads just added. Pick up 1 B bead, one 2-mm crystal bead, and 1 B bead. Pass through the D bead opposite the one you originally exited. Pick up 1 B bead, one 2-mm crystal bead, and 1 B bead. Pass through the first D bead you exited. Pass through the first group of side beads, the D bead, the second group of side beads, and the next D bead. Add an additional group of side beads and pass through the opposite D bead. Weave in the thread and trim. Repeat the embellishment on the opposite side of the band (figure 10).

Weave the thread to an edge bead on the ring mount. Pick up 1 B bead and pass through the next edge bead. Repeat around all 4 edges of the ring mount. Repeat to embellish the edge of the ring top's base using C beads (figure 11).

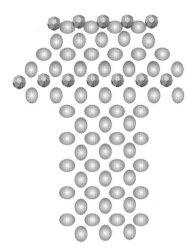

figure 8

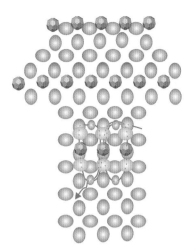

figure 10

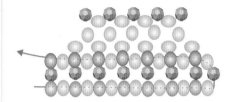

figure 11

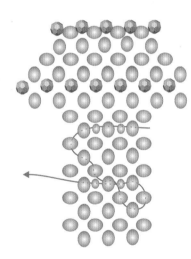

figure 9

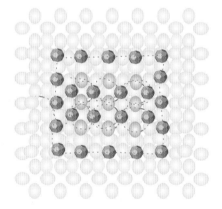

figure 6

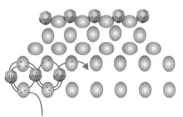

figure 7

115

SERENA

The body of this bracelet is all about texture and sparkle. The striped effect is created by building up a second layer of right angle weave strips from the base of the piece.

▶ 1. Base

Use A beads to stitch a strip of right angle weave 8 units wide and 55 rows long, or an odd number of rows long enough to fit your wrist minus the width of the clasp.

Continued on next page

Continued on next page

117

▶ 2. 90-Degree Rows

Orient the strip so one of the short edges points up. Weave through the beads to exit from the right-hand top bead. Pick up 3 B beads and make a counterclockwise circle to pass through the A bead you just exited. Pass through the side bead, top bead, and side bead just added and the next top A bead at the edge of the base. Pick up 2 B beads and pass clockwise through the side bead from the first B-bead unit, the second base A bead, and the new side A bead. Repeat across the row. This row should stand up at a 90-degree angle to the base row. To step up to the next row, pass through a side and top bead in the base row.

Repeat to add right angle weave units to each row of beads whose holes are horizontal (the top and bottom beads in your base strip). Remember that the first unit will always have 3 beads and subsequent units will have 2 beads (figure 1).

▶ 3. Join Rows

Weave through beads to exit from the top left-hand bead of the last layer 2 row. Join this row to the next layered row using C beads (see figure 20 in Fundamentals, page 23). When the join is complete, pass through the side bead in the layered unit, an edge bead on the base, the side bead in the next layered unit, and exit from the first top bead in the next row. Join the next row using size 3-mm bicone crystals.
Note: The space between the layered rows 2 and 3 will be unjoined, as will every other space between 2 layered rows. Repeat, alternating the joins between the size 11° beads and the 3-mm bicone crystals until all layered rows have been joined (figure 2).

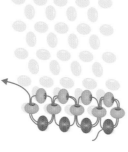

figure 1

▶ 4. Clasp

Orient the bracelet so one short edge points up. Weave through the beads to exit up through the second side bead on the edge. Pick up 7 size 15° beads, pass through the first loop on one half of the clasp, and pass back through the side bead. Weave through the beadwork to exit up through the side bead opposite the middle loop on the clasp and repeat. Repeat once more for the third attachment point. Attach the second slide component to the other end in the same way (figure 3).

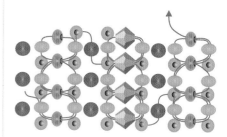

figure 2

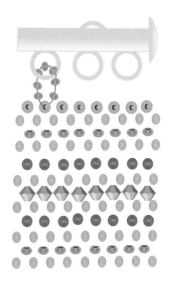

figure 3

GALLERY

This section of work by bead artists spotlights the versatility of right angle weave, showcasing purses, scarves, and sculptures, as well as jewelry.

TOP RIGHT

Tina Hauer

Golden Circle, 2007

8.9 x 8.9 cm

Seed beads, crystal bicones; circular right angle weave

PHOTO BY MARCIA DECOSTER

TOP LEFT

Daeng Weaver

Untitled, 2005

3.8 x 2.5 x 3.8 cm

Crystals, seed beads; right angle weave, embellished

PHOTO BY MARCIA DECOSTER

LEFT CENTER

Daeng Weaver

Untitled, 2003

45.7 cm long

Tourmaline beads, crystals, seed beads, wire; right angle weave, wire wrapping

PHOTO BY MARCIA DECOSTER

BOTTOM

Shelley Nybakke

Metalsmith's Match, 2007

Outer diameter, 26 cm

Metal seed beads; right angle weave

PHOTO BY CHAD JONES

TOP

Nan C. Meinhardt

"Balls, Balls," Said the Queen, 2007

61 x 15.2 x 2.5 cm

Glass seed beads, 24-karat gold seed
beads, paint, wood; right angle weave

PHOTOS BY TOM VAN EYNDE

CENTER

Rachel Nelson-Smith

*O. Bersten Component Bracelet
Pink and Green,* 2007

1.6 x 3.8 x 17.8 cm

Japanese seed beads and drops,
Swarovski crystals, gold-filled findings,
vintage clasp; modified right angle weave,
peyote stitch, tubular even-count peyote
stitch, embellished

PHOTO BY ARTIST

BOTTOM

Sandra Jaech

Pyramid Pod, 2004

14 x 15.2 x 15.2 cm

Seed beads, silk, Ultrasuede; right angle
weave, peyote brick stitch,
embroidery stitch

PHOTO BY ARTIST

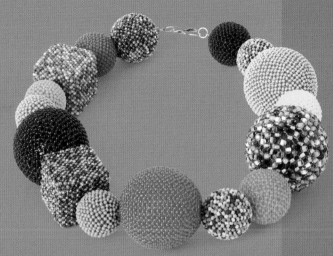

TOP LEFT

Suzanne Golden

Sweet Hearts, 2007

63.5 cm long

Swarovski crystals, Swarovski glass
sequins, 24-karat gold, seed beads;
right angle weave

PHOTO BY LARRY SANDERS

TOP RIGHT

Stacy Creamer

Primarily Primaries, 2005

43.2 cm long

Seed beads, painted wooden
beads; right angle weave

PHOTO BY ARTIST

BOTTOM

Rachel Nelson-Smith

Ootheca Cuff Turquoise, 2006

4.4 x 8.3 x 8.3 cm

Japanese seed beads, Swarovski
crystals, niobium wire, sterling-
silver magnetic clasps; right-angle
weave, tubular even-count peyote
stitch, wire work

PHOTO BY ARTIST

Betsy Perdue

Circa 540 AD, 2007

30.5 x 15.2 x 3.2 cm

Seed beads, sterling-silver beads, fringe, steel armature fabricated by Dave Keyes; right angle weave, Ndebele beadwork

PHOTO BY ARTIST

BOTTOM LEFT

Sandra Jaech

Bird's Nest, 2007

12.7 x 20.3 x 12.7 cm

Seed beads, coral, mother-of-pearl; right angle weave, square stitch

PHOTO BY ARTIST

BOTTOM RIGHT

Daeng Weaver

Untitled, 2004

17.8 x 3.8 cm

Crystals, seed beads; right angle weave

PHOTO BY MARCIA DECOSTER

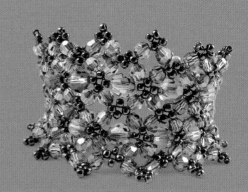

**Marcia DeCoster and the
Dallas Bead Society**

Chorus of Urchins, 2008

5.1 x 40.6 cm

Seed beads, Swarovski crystals; right
angle weave, peyote stitch

PHOTO BY MARCIA DECOSTER

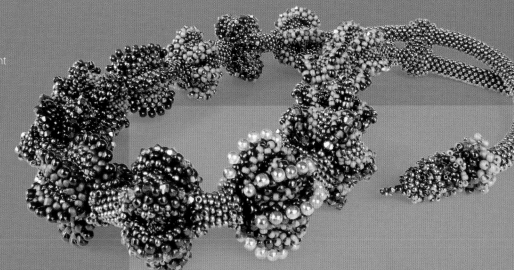

BOTTOM LEFT

Huib Petersen

Going Medieval, 2008

2.5 x 2.5 x 40.6 cm

Seed beads, crystals, faceted glass
beads; tubular right angle weave

PHOTO BY ARTIST

BOTTOM RIGHT

Susan Blessinger

Contemporary Collar, 2008

40.6 x 20.3 x 0.6 cm

Rondelles, Swarovski bicones, seed
beads; right angle weave

PHOTO BY MARCIA DECOSTER

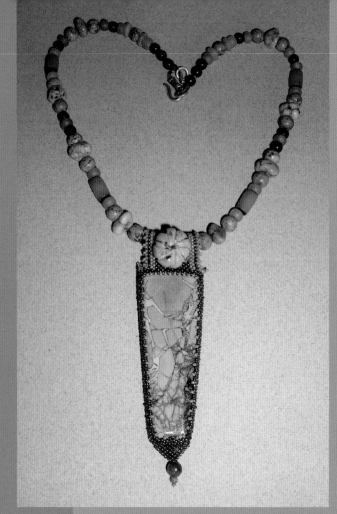

124

TOP LEFT

Sandra Jaech

*Raw-Bezeled Royston
Turquoise Pendant,* 2004

31.8 x 3.2 x 1.3 cm

Royston turquoise cabochon, seed
beads; right angle weave

PHOTO BY ARTIST

TOP RIGHT

Maggie Meister

Pelta Necklace, 2007

17.8 x 27.9 cm

Seed beads, sterling silver beads, semiprecious stones; right angle weave

PHOTO BY LARRY SANDERS

BOTTOM

Jeannette Cook

Falling Leaves Scarf, 2007

83.8 x 10.2 cm

Delica beads, seed beads;
right angle weave, peyote stitch

PHOTO BY MELINDA HOLDEN

TOP LEFT
Huib Petersen
My Father's Watchband, 2005
3.2 x 1.9 x 21.6 cm
Seed beads; tubular right angle weave
PHOTO BY ARTIST

TOP RIGHT
Stacy Creamer
Homage to David Chatt Cuff, 2005
19.1 x 5.1 cm
Seed beads; single-needle right angle weave
PHOTO BY ARTIST

BOTTOM
Eleanor N. Wirth
Towers of Power, 2008
14 x 8.9 cm
Seed beads, Swarovski crystals;
right angle weave, square stitch
PHOTO BY MARCIA DECOSTER

TOP LEFT

Ana Maria Garcia

Red Heart Pouch, 2008

38.1 x 15.2 x 2.5 cm

Seed beads, wire frame;
right angle weave

PHOTO BY TIM HARDING

TOP RIGHT

Kelly J. Angeley

Diatoms, 2007

52 x 2 x 2.5 cm

Seed beads, crystals, glass bead
lampworked by George O'Grady;
right angle weave

PHOTO BY BARRY JENSEN

BOTTOM

Rachel Nelson-Smith

*O. Bersten Component Bracelet
for Pat H.*, 2007

1.6 x 3.8 x 17.8 cm

Japanese seed beads, Swarovski crystals, sterling silver; modified right angle
weave, peyote bezel, tubular even-
count peyote stitch, embellished

PHOTO BY ARTIST

ABOUT THE AUTHOR

A love for beautiful jewelry and a lifelong passion to create brought Marcia DeCoster to beads in the early 1990s. As she gained proficiency and her designs became more original, Marcia began teaching workshops in the United States and internationally. Her classes focus on designing with right angle weave.

She lives with her husband, Mark, in California. With his support and encouragement, Marcia became a full-time bead artist in 2004. For someone who loves beading, jewelry, travel, and people, it's the ideal career. The couple raised their three children in Santa Cruz and now shares an Art Deco home in San Diego with Miss Princess Maya Angelina DeCoster, their adorable dog.

Marcia's designs have appeared in various publications, including *Beadwork, Bead and Button, The Beader's Color Palette* by Margie Deeb, and *The Complete Guide to Beading Techniques* by Jane Davis. She has jewelry in Carol Wilcox Wells' book *The Art and Elegance of Beadweaving* (Lark Books, 2003), and her work is also showcased in *Masters: Beadweaving* (Lark Books, 2008).

ACKNOWLEDGMENTS

I'm fortunate to have so many incredibly talented and giving folks in my life. Each of them made a difference in bringing this book into being.

My dear husband, Mark, took the time to learn right angle weave so I could observe a non-beader learning the stitch. This is only one of the many ways in which he supports me.

Bonnie Brooks, a bead illustrator of great talent, was so gracious in sharing her knowledge. I can't imagine how I could have done it without her.

I'm grateful to the community of bead artists whose friendship provides a source of constant support. When the process seemed long, I could always count on Jeannette Cook, Rachel Nelson-Smith, Arlene Watson, Annie Hesse, Susan Kazarian, and Jonna Faulkner to respond to e-mails with just the right words.

A great number of beaders were responsible for providing invaluable feedback during the design and illustration phase. Thanks go to Tina Hauer, Linda Torgensen, Liz Thompson, Lisa Garoon, Nancy Kvorka, Michelle Link, Susan Blessinger, Susan Lynch, Dyan Bender, Katie Nelson, Laura Garber, Eleanor Wirth, Gabriella Van Diepen, Carolyn Slater, Kelly Angeley, Nan Halberg, Shelly Rontal, Joan Endsley, Sandy Martin, and Lexi Schwartz.

My journey with beads has been amazing, and made more so by all the wonderful bead-store owners who shared their knowledge and gave me guidance throughout the years. Your belief in me meant everything, and I thank you!

To all the beaders who have put their faith in my teaching by choosing to take my class, I am honored. From each of you I continue to learn and to be inspired by your color choices, your talent, and your own beading voice.

Jean Campbell contributed her considerable expertise as the copy editor for this book. Chevron Trading Post & Bead Co., an outstanding bead store in downtown Asheville, North Carolina, graciously loaned beading supplies to photograph for the beading kit. Chris Hunter of 828:design contributed his terrific graphic sensibilities in laying out the book.

Finally, I appreciate the many people at Lark Books who provided answers when I needed them and who guided me through the process. Thank you, Ray Hemachandra, Nathalie Mornu, and Dana Irwin. Thanks also to Dawn Dillingham, Kathleen McCafferty, and Beth Sweet.

Susan Kazarian
Raw Scallops, 2007
2.5 x 17.8 x 1 cm
Swarovski crystals; right angle weave
PHOTO BY RACHEL NELSON-SMITH

INDEX